ZAYN MALIK

ZAYN MALIK

MALIK

THE BIOGRAPHY

SARAH OLIVER

JOHN BLAKE

Published by John Blake Publishing Ltd,
3 Bramber Court, 2 Bramber Road,
London W14 9PB, England

www.johnblakepublishing.co.uk

www.facebook.com/Johnblakepub [facebook]
twitter.com/johnblakepub [twitter]

This edition published in 2014

ISBN: 978 1 78219 751 5

British Library Cataloguing-in-Publication Data:

A catalogue record for this book is available from the British Library.

Design by www.envydesign.co.uk

Printed and bound in Great Britain by CPI Group (UK) Ltd

1 3 5 7 9 10 8 6 4 2

Papers used by John Blake Publishing are natural, recyclable products made
from wood grown in sustainable forests. The manufacturing processes conform
to the environmental regulations of the country of origin.

Every attempt has been made to contact the relevant copyright-holders, but some
were unobtainable. We would be grateful if the appropriate people could contact us.

ABOUT THE AUTHOR

Sarah Oliver is a writer from Widnes in Cheshire. She was the author of the first ever book on Zayn, Niall, Liam, Louis and Harry, entitled *One Direction A–Z*, which was a *Sunday Times* bestseller. She also wrote the double biography of Harry Styles and Niall Horan, the book *One Direction Around the World*, and appeared in the documentary *One Direction – All For One*. Why not follow Sarah – @SarahOliverAtoZ – on Twitter?

Dedicated with love to Courtney and Lizzy

CONTENTS

If you love One Direction then you should follow the boys on Twitter. Here are the Twitter addresses you need:

One Direction – http://twitter.com/onedirection

Zayn – https://twitter.com/zaynmalik

Harry – http://twitter.com/harry_styles

Niall – https://twitter.com/NiallOfficial

Louis – https://twitter.com/Louis_Tomlinson

Liam – https://twitter.com/Real_Liam_Payne

CHAPTER ONE

1993: A STAR IS BORN!

Zayn is from East Bowling in Bradford and he was born on 12 January 1993 at St Luke's Hospital, Bradford. He is the second oldest member of One Direction – only Louis is older than him. His dad is called Yaser and his mum is called Trisha. They were so excited when he was born – he was their first son and a great playmate for little Doniya, who was one at the time. Zayn's wider family were really happy too.

Yaser and Trisha gave him the middle name Javadd. They spelt his first name Zain and when Zayn was on *The X Factor* he was referred to as Zain but he prefers it to be spelt Zayn, so after the show he made sure that he would be known as Zayn from then on.

> **DID YOU KNOW?**
> Zayn means 'beautiful' in Arabic and Malik, his surname, means 'king' or 'chieftain'.

When Zayn was growing up he was always full of energy. He loved being the centre of attention and he liked to sing and dance. His parents had two more children after Zayn: Waliyha and Safaa. Waliyha is six years younger and Safaa is ten years Zayn's junior, but the family are all still very close.

Zayn would put on shows for his parents and, as he grew up, he kept on performing for them, along with his sisters. He would do his own versions of Daniel Bedingfield tracks like 'If You're Not The One' and dreamed of performing on stage. His mum admitted to the *Mirror*: 'I have quite a few videos of him singing as a little boy but he's banned me from showing anyone. My favourite is him singing "I Believe I Can Fly" [By R. Kelly] wearing a green dressing gown.'

> **DID YOU KNOW?**
> Zayn says the one thing that's guaranteed to make him smile is talking to his little sister Safaa.

Zayn is close to his dad, who looked after him before he went to school. Zayn was very hyperactive so Yaser had his hands full! Both Zayn and his dad love drawing and art.

> **DID YOU KNOW?**
> When 1D were being interviewed for *You Generation* Zayn was challenged to draw a picture of his favourite member of One Direction in one minute. He chose Louis and the sketch he did was really good. In the same inter-

view Niall did a brilliant impression of Zayn. Check it out on YouTube.

Even though Zayn didn't go to nursery he was still really excited about starting primary school. He liked playing in the sand with the other children and listening to his teacher read stories to the class. He was small for his age but very intelligent. By the time he was in junior school he could read difficult books that even teenagers might have struggled with. Back home, he practised reading a lot with his grandad, who encouraged him to push himself.

But school wasn't always a happy place for Zayn. Often he felt like the odd one out because there were no other children like him. No one else was of mixed heritage (Zayn's dad is British Pakistani and his mum is half Irish and half English). Zayn only stayed at his first primary school for two years before moving to another school where he was much happier. He met his best friend Sam at Lower Fields Primary School and they had lots of fun together until they moved schools and drifted apart.

DID YOU KNOW?

When Zayn was younger he had two cats called Lily and Lolo and a Staffordshire bull terrier called Tyson. The Malik family now have two cats called Rolo and Tom and a dog named Boris.

Zayn ended up going to lots of different schools, for a whole host of different reasons. He admitted to *Sugar* magazine: 'I got expelled from a couple of schools for fighting.

'Where I'm from, you kind of had to get into a couple of scrapes to survive.'

While at Tong High School, Zayn was caught with a BB gun in school and got into lots of trouble. He hadn't fired it at anyone but that didn't matter, his teachers still had to punish him for having an imitation firearm.

Whenever he started at a new school he would get lots of attention from girls, who wanted to know everything about him because he was new, which made Zayn feel cool. He liked getting extra attention.

Zayn has always loved singing and one of his earliest gigs was while he was a pupil at Lower Fields Primary School and he sang in a choir for the Lord Mayor at his local supermarket. At Tong High School Zayn combined singing with acting when he played the title role in their production of *Bugsy Malone*. He didn't get nervous although he sang in front of 400 people in the audience. Zayn also appeared in the school's production of *The Arabian Nights* and had a part created for him in the musical *Grease*. He wasn't old enough to be a T-Bird so his teacher created a young T-Bird part for him and one for his friend Aqib Khan.

DID YOU KNOW?

Aqib Khan is now a professional actor and played Sajid Khan in the 2010 film *West Is West* and Rashid Jarwar in the ITV series *The Jury II*. If you search on YouTube, you can see a short clip of Zayn and Aqib in *Grease* – they both look really young.

When he was in high school acting was Zayn's real passion and singing was his second love. He joined the school choir at the request of his teacher Mrs Fox, who thought he had a good voice. Around this time Zayn became best friends with a boy called Danny, who was in his drama class, and also befriended

1993: A STAR IS BORN!

Danny's younger brother, Anthony. Today, they are still close and chill out with each other whenever Zayn is home. They love playing on the Xbox together and share the same sense of humour. If you google Zayn Malik, Anthony Riach & Danny Riach Dancing you will see a cool video of the three of them dancing to an Usher song – and boy, can they dance!

DID YOU KNOW?

Zayn's three favourite subjects at school were English, art and drama. He really excelled at them, as Steve Gates, assistant head teacher at Tong High, told the *Telegraph & Argus*: 'Zayn is a model student who excelled in all the performing arts subjects, one of the specialist subjects here at Tong.

'He was always a star performer in all the school productions so it was no surprise when Simon Cowell threw him his big chance.'

One day when Zayn was at school he was given the opportunity to sing with British singer–songwriter/rapper Jay Sean. Jay remembers the day well and explained to 2DAY FM in June 2012: 'About five years ago I happened to be at a school in England and I was doing, like, these talks about music and who wants to be a musician and blah, blah, blah. So anyway, I was on stage singing and then I went out to the crowd and I was like, "Are there any aspiring singers over here?" and then this little boy puts his hand up and I was like, "You, come up here, man!" and I was like, "Have you ever sung before?" and he was like, "No, I'm really shy, I'm really nervous," and I was like, "Listen, we're going to do this together. We're going to sing one of my songs and we're going to do it together, me and you."'

Jay Sean and Zayn sang the song 'Ride It' and the experience was to leave a lasting impression on Zayn. It was the first time he had sung on stage and it really boosted his confidence. Recently, Zayn tweeted Jay Sean to ask him if he remembered that day, and to say a big thank you.

DID YOU KNOW?

Zayn was so good at English that he sat his GCSE English exam a year early.

In the summer before starting at sixth-form college Zayn grew a lot so he was no longer small for his age. Some of his classmates were really shocked when they saw him in September – he looked like a new person, he had grown so much. He had started boxing in his spare time and confessed to the *Daily Star*: 'I did boxing from when I was 15 to 17. I love it and I've started training again now on the side, even though we don't get much time off for exercise.

'I'm trying to eat healthier so I can bulk up. I'd love to pursue it properly one day.'

DID YOU KNOW?

Zayn loves cats and his favourite animals are lions. If he were an animal, he would like to be a monkey. Also, at school and college Zayn's nickname was 'Z' (pronounced 'Zed').

CHAPTER TWO

TIME TO SHINE

Zayn would never have auditioned for *The X Factor* if had not been for his music teacher, who told him to go for it. For two years he had the application form but never sent it in – he was just too nervous. Zayn auditioned in Manchester and was given the number 165616 when he registered. He nearly backed out but his mum encouraged him, with Zayn admitting to the *Telegraph & Argus* newspaper: 'I was really nervous but she told me just to get on with it and not miss my chance.' If it wasn't for Trisha, Zayn could have missed out on the opportunity to be in One Direction.

DID YOU KNOW?

Here are the other boys' audition numbers: Louis – 155204, Liam – 61898, Niall – 232677 and Harry – 165998.

The first people that Zayn had to impress weren't the judges but the backstage production team. They judge everyone before choosing their favourites to return on a second day to sing for Simon Cowell, Nicole Scherzinger and Louis Walsh. Thousands of people wanted to get through so Zayn had his work cut out to impress the production team. They only pick the very best (and the absolute worst) singers to make it through to the next round. Zayn was over the moon when he was told he was good enough, and his family were very proud. All he had to do now was make sure his nerves didn't get the better of him.

Zayn chose to sing 'Let Me Love You' by Mario. He decided to dress casually for his audition rather than wear something too smart. Backstage, his proud mum, dad and sister waited with host Dermot O'Leary and they clapped every time they heard a judge say 'Yes'. Zayn got a yes from all three judges so he knew he was going through to *X Factor* Bootcamp!

It was really disappointing for Zayn's family and friends that his audition was missed from *The X Factor* and *Xtra Factor* audition shows when they were shown on television. Only Harry and Liam's auditions made *The X Factor* audition shows and Niall's performance was shown on *The Xtra Factor* one. Louis also missed out. At this stage *The X Factor* producers couldn't have thought that Zayn and Louis were going to make the live shows and decided to showcase other singers instead. Poor Zayn, he had done so well in his audition and he deserved to have his performance shown.

DID YOU KNOW?

Some One Direction fans started an online petition to get Zayn's and Louis' auditions aired on TV or put on YouTube and it worked. After the final was over, their auditions were broadcast on TV for the very first time and fans could see how well Zayn did.

Zayn did so well standing on stage and singing for the judges in his first audition because there were thousands of people watching in the audience. He needed to impress them as well as the judges, so he had to try and hide his shyness. Because Zayn has performed non-stop since *The X Factor*, these days he is a lot less withdrawn but he still has his shy moments. He would describe himself as 'the shy one' out of all the boys. In an interview for VEVO he said: 'Before *X Factor* I'd never done anything that required me to have to speak in front of cameras or in front of people. *The X Factor* kinda helped me with that because you're followed around by cameras and you get used to it.'

Zayn never thought he'd make it to the finals of *The X Factor*. He entered the show 'just for the experience.'

For the Bootcamp stage Zayn had to head for London, leaving his family behind. From that time on, things were going to be even tougher because the judges had chosen only really great singers to make it through. Bootcamp was held at Wembley Arena over five days in July 2010 to whittle down the 211 acts that had survived the first round. All the singers had to be at the Arena early on 22 July because they had a lot to fit in. Zayn had to stand with the other lads, as he would be in the Boys' category if he made it through. The Boys were told to practise 'Man In The Mirror' by Michael Jackson. The Girls had to practise Beyoncé's 'If I Were A Boy', while the Groups practised 'Nothing's Gonna Stop Us Now' by Starship, and the Over-25s had to sing Lady Gaga's 'Poker Face'. At this stage none of the contestants' first auditions had been shown on TV so Zayn had no idea who the favourites in the Boys' category were.

He must have been feeling nervous when Simon Cowell told all the singers: 'By the end of the day, half of you are going home. Today you're going to be put into your categories and you're going to sing one song. There are literally no second chances today.'

Zayn really didn't want to be on the train back to Bradford that night and so he had to make his version of 'Man In The Mirror' really stand out from the other hopefuls. He was under a lot of pressure, but this is what Simon and Louis Walsh were after: they wanted to push these aspiring pop stars hard to get the best out of them. In their first auditions the singers had been able to choose any song they liked, but their first Bootcamp song had to be something selected for them.

Zayn did really well – his performance of 'Man In The Mirror' was great and he showed the judges what a talented singer he was. Other singers failed to perform to his level and some even struggled to remember the lyrics. Harry, Liam, Louis and Niall also did well at this stage but because they were all auditioning as solo artists at this point they were competing against each other.

Zayn was thrilled when he was told that he was to come back for Day 2: he had made the next round and wouldn't be going home that night. He knew that Day 2 would be even tougher, though, because already so many good singers had been told to leave. After he rang his family to let them know Day 1 had been a success, he then tried to get some sleep.

On arrival at Wembley the next day Zayn and all the remaining singers were instructed to go to the stage. Simon and Louis introduced them to Brian Friedman, international choreographer and dancer, who would be teaching them how to dance. Brian is one of the best choreographers in the world and has worked with Britney Spears, Beyoncé and Mariah Carey among others.

Brian told the singers: 'I don't want you to be scared. What we are going to work on is your stage presence and choreography.'

There had never been a dance element at Bootcamp before so Simon and the other judges had no idea what it would be like, but they wanted to challenge the contestants to try something new. Simon reassured the singers that no one would be eliminated if their dancing skills weren't up to scratch but they still had to give 110 per cent.

Zayn tried his best in rehearsals but he struggled to pick up the choreography and it made him feel like a failure. He felt he was so bad that he couldn't perform in front of Simon. When the boys were called on stage to show the judges what they had learnt, Zayn stayed backstage and he must have thought that his *X Factor* dream was over. Simon, Louis and Brian watched the boys dance, picking out their favourite dancers. Before Brian could dismiss the boys and call on the next group of dancers, though, Simon asked him where Zayn was – he had noticed that he was missing. At first Brian didn't know but after asking, he discovered that Zayn was backstage, refusing to come out. Simon decided that they couldn't go on without Zayn so personally went backstage to ask him to dance.

Zayn told the backstage camera: 'I seriously don't want to do it because I hate dancing and I've never done it before, and I feel like an idiot on the stage with other people who are clearly better than me and I just feel like an idiot – I'm not doing it.

'I just know I'm going to do it wrong because I don't know it. When you've got to perform in front of Simon and professionals that know what they're doing and how to dance, and professional choreographers and stuff, and I just don't know…'

Normally Simon would have had no time for someone who refuses to do what he wants him to do but he felt like he had to help Zayn. He had been impressed by the young man's singing the day before and didn't want him to make the biggest mistake of his life and leave because of his reluctance to dance. This was the kind of decision that Zayn could end up regretting for the rest of his life.

Simon asked him: 'Zayn, why aren't you out there? Why aren't you out there? You can't just bottle it… you can't just hide behind here. Zayn, you are ruining this for yourself! I'm trying to help you here. So if you can't do it now, you'll never gonna be able to do it, right? Come on, let's go and do it.'

Zayn couldn't ignore Simon's advice and so he decided to give it a go. Just before he went on stage, Simon said: 'Don't do that again, get on with it.' They quickly shook hands and Simon went back to his position next to Louis and Brian.

Simon allowed Harry and a few of the other boys to dance again with Zayn so that he wouldn't have to do it on his own. Zayn wasn't great but he wasn't that bad and although Simon thought he looked 'uncomfortable', he was impressed that Zayn had tried. Afterwards, the reluctant dancer must have been relieved that it was all over and he told the cameras that he would work on his dancing skills and his confidence levels.

On the third day of Bootcamp Zayn and the other contestants met the third judge, former Pussycat Dolls' singer Nicole Scherzinger. She had been impressed with Zayn after his first audition but he knew that he must impress her again if he was to make the 'Judges' Houses' round. Nicole was a surprise addition because the third Bootcamp judge was supposed to be former Girls Aloud singer Cheryl Cole but she was recovering from malaria so couldn't be there. She had contracted the disease after climbing Mount Kilimanjaro to raise money for charity. Nicole would simply be taking Cheryl's place at Bootcamp, and Cheryl would hopefully be back soon.

Because of the changes to the judges' line-up, *The X Factor* producers chose to cancel the live element of Bootcamp. They tweeted: 'Due to the unusual circumstances, we are not inviting an audience to watch the contestants perform at *The X Factor* boot camp.' Although this announcement disappointed thousands of people who had been looking forward to catching a first glimpse of the contestants it must have helped the Bootcamp residents, who were no doubt feeling nervous and lacking in confidence. Zayn could simply concentrate on impressing Simon, Louis and Nicole – the three judges who had given him three 'yeses' in the first audition round – rather than thinking of the thousands of people watching in the arena.

For their final performances the singers were given a list of 40 songs and told to find one number to sing that would showcase their voice. No one could afford to pick the wrong song and they couldn't make too 'safe' a choice, because they were required to perform it in a different slant, treating it in their own unique way. Zayn chose 'Make You Feel My Love' by Adele/Bob Dylan, which incidentally is the exact same song that Louis chose to sing!

After Zayn had performed it must have been hard as he made his way backstage because the judges didn't give any feedback at all, they just said 'thanks' and there was no hint of what they thought in their facial expressions. All Zayn and the other contestants could do was go back to the hotel and try to sleep – the next day the judges would be deciding who would be going through to Judges' Houses, so the wannabe pop stars had an anxious wait ahead.

It might have been tough on Zayn and the other singers but the fifth and final day of Bootcamp was tough on the judges too because there had been so many talented singers that it really was hard to pick just six in each category to make it through. In the end they decided to choose eight singers for each category and to slightly adjust the older category so that it was Over-28s instead of Over-25s.

There were 30 talented boys left in the competition so the atmosphere was tense when they were called onto the stage to find out their fate. As the judges started calling out the names of the singers who had made it through, Zayn was incredibly nervous.

Simon was the first to speak, saying: 'The first person through to the Judges' Houses is… John Wilding.'

Nicole: 'Nicolo Festa.'

Louis: 'Paije Richardson.'

Simon: 'Aiden Grimshaw.'

Louis: 'Marlon McKenzie.'

Louis: 'Karl Brown.'

Nicole: 'Matt Cardle.'

Simon Cowell: 'The final contestant who's made it through is Tom Richards… That's it, guys – I'm really sorry.'

To get so close and then to be rejected was really hard for Zayn to take – he had wanted to perform on *The X Factor* stage so much. Of course the other singers who failed to get through were equally gutted. Liam, Niall and Harry were so upset that they were crying. Liam told host Dermot O'Leary: 'I just don't want to go home. I just don't want to go!'

Niall said that it was one of the worst things he'd ever had to do in his life – 'standing there, waiting for your name to be called, and then it's not.'

All that was left for them to do was to collect their belongings before leaving the arena. But just before they could go a member of the production team came and asked Zayn, Liam, Louis, Niall and Harry to go and wait on the stage alongside four girls: Sophia Wardman, Geneva Lane, Esther Campbell and Rebecca Creighton. Zayn didn't know what was happening but he hoped they were about to be given a second chance – he was right. Nicole Scherzinger was the first to speak once they had lined up on stage, with Zayn in the middle: 'Hello, thank you so much for coming back. Judging from some of your faces, this is really hard. We've thought long and hard about it and we've thought of each of you as individuals, and we just feel that you're too talented to let go of. We think it would be a great idea to have two separate groups.' Simon teased that they should form groups and that they might meet again in the future, before saying: 'We've decided to put you both through… This is a lifeline – you've got to work ten, twelve, fourteen hours a day, every single day and take this opportunity. You've got a real shot here, guys.' Up until then it was sounding like the judges wanted them to audition the following year. Zayn's dream wasn't over yet!

The boys had to have a think and decide whether they wanted to form a group but Zayn's mind was made up, he wanted to give it a go. He told American talk show host Barbara Walters in December 2012: 'It was a no-brainer – we just wanted to see how far we could get in the competition, and so we were like, "Cool, let's give it a go."'

Even though the boys found out in July that they had made it through to the Judges' Houses round, they were sworn to secrecy so they couldn't tell their friends. They had to keep quiet for months as the Bootcamp episodes were not being shown on TV until Saturday, 2 and Sunday, 3 October 2010.

CHAPTER THREE

IMPRESSING SIMON

The boys didn't find out who would be their judge until after Bootcamp. It could have been Louis Walsh, Dannii Minogue, Cheryl Cole or Simon Cowell, but the judge they really wanted was Simon because of his experience. The boys got their wish, but this meant they really had to work hard in the weeks leading up to Judges' Houses because Simon is a really hard judge to impress.

DID YOU KNOW?

Initially Simon was disappointed that he was given the Groups' category as his first choice was the Girls' category and his second choice was the Boys. He had no idea how strong Zayn, Harry, Louis, Liam and Niall were because he had yet to see them perform together.

From day one Zayn, Harry, Louis, Liam and Niall were determined that they were going to succeed and make *The X Factor* live shows. In previous series' of *The X Factor* when the judges had formed groups often they had felt disappointed by the result, even though the group members had been offered a lifeline. Zayn, Harry, Louis, Liam and Niall knew that the standard of groups that had made the Judges' Houses round was high so they had to rehearse like crazy to make sure they were the best. They were keen for Simon to forget that he had just formed them when they sang, they wanted to sound like they had been singing together for years.

Just a few days after returning home from Bootcamp Niall, Liam and Louis made their way to Harry's home in Holmes Chapel, Cheshire. His mum (Anne Cox) had offered to have them stay for a few weeks. Zayn had commitments at home so couldn't be there for the first three days but the second he could, he got there. Because it was the summer holidays Zayn didn't have to miss college and so he could tell people at home that he was going on holiday – he couldn't reveal how far he had got in the competition.

It actually worked out well that the boys were from different parts of England (and Ireland) because it made them commit to spending twenty-four hours a day with each other at Harry's home. Had they lived locally they might have met up only in the daytime and then gone home in the evenings, but because they were far away from home, they had no alternative but to stay together. In fact they ended up spending almost three weeks in each other's company, rehearsing and getting to know each other. Zayn found the time intense but got to see the best and worst parts of Harry, Liam, Niall and Louis and this ultimately helped him bond with all the boys.

DID YOU KNOW?

Because Zayn was the last to arrive, to begin with he felt a bit like the odd one out. During their time at Harry's home, the boys rehearsed songs by Jay Sean and Jason Derulo.

The boys did enjoy themselves during their time at Harry's home but they also made sure they rehearsed too. They had their fair share of petty squabbles but that was to be expected as they had only just met each other at Bootcamp. Because Zayn, Harry, Niall, Liam and Louis had each entered the competition as solo artists, they each had their own ideas about the type of singer they wanted to be and the kind of songs they wanted to sing. That said, they knew Simon would be choosing their song for Judges' Houses so the decision was out of their control. They just needed to work on their harmonies and figure out who would be the best to sing the lead vocals – not an easy thing to decide because they were all equally talented. Each one tried out different roles, and after much discussion they found their places in the overall group.

DID YOU KNOW?

Zayn had different musical tastes to the others in the beginning. He loved hip-hop and R&B, as he explained to Billboard.com: 'I had kind of pigeonholed myself a little bit, so I was very aware that the guys had different musical tastes. It really broadened my taste. I listen to a lot more different stuff now – Kings of Leon, The Script. I think there's so many great bands out there I hadn't really heard before and now I get to listen to them.'

During the weeks leading up to Judges' Houses the boys had to come up with a name for their group that summed up who they were and what they were about. It was really difficult because they didn't want a name that sounded silly or had no meaning behind it. Zayn, Niall, Liam and Louis all racked their brains but it was Harry who came up with One Direction quite by accident, it just popped into his head. The other boys thought it was a great name as they all wanted the same thing, and they were all going in one direction – straight to the top of the charts!

For the Judges' Houses round the boys needed one unified look that would make them look like a group, without seeming like clones of one another. They chatted about what they might wear and then decided to wear grey or white pumps, casual shorts or three-quarter trousers with loose-fitting shirts or T-shirts. Zayn wore blue trousers with a white T-shirt.

For Zayn, waiting in the airport for their flight to Spain felt strange because he had never been abroad before. They would be competing against seven other groups in the following days so the pressure was certainly on. Thankfully, the boys all had each other for support and their mums were only at the other end of the phone if they needed to ask their advice or if they got homesick.

DID YOU KNOW?

Before *The X Factor* the furthest Zayn had ever been away from home was Birmingham – and that's just 88 miles away from Bradford!

When the boys landed, they were driven to Simon's rented villa in Marbella – their new temporary home. They found it hard to take in how grand the place was: there were three swimming pools, twenty bedrooms, a cinema and so much more. It was like nothing they had ever seen before.

One day when they visited the beach Louis was stung by a sea urchin and ended up being rushed to hospital. All the boys were worried about their friend and couldn't help but think that they might have to perform as a four-piece band. Zayn told *The X Factor* cameras: 'We're all panicking a little bit 'cos we're not sure what's going to happen or when he's going to get here.' Liam added: 'For us that's really bad as we haven't had that much time to practise as we've only just got together as a group. I hope he's back as we really do need him.'

Luckily, Louis wasn't kept in hospital and was allowed to return to Simon's villa just in time for the boys' performance. Zayn, Harry, Niall, Liam and Louis performed 'Torn', a ballad by Natalie Imbruglia. Liam sang the verse, Harry took on the chorus, Niall and Louis harmonised and Zayn finished the song perfectly. Despite their nerves it couldn't have gone any better. After finishing the song the boys had to leave the performance area and just wait to find out if they had done enough. Once the boys were out of earshot, Simon told his helper Sinitta: 'They're cool, they're relevant.'

Harry summed up how all the boys were feeling, telling *The X Factor* cameras: 'Your hunger for it grows and grows as you get through each stage in the competition. It's just the biggest stage to be told yes or no. It's one word that can change your life forever because it won't be the same if you get a "yes" and if you get a "no" then it's straight back to doing stuff that kind of drives you to come here in the first place.'

ONE DIRECTION'S RIVALS AND THE
SONGS THEY SANG AT JUDGES' HOUSES

Belle Amie sang 'Faith' by George Michael
Diva Fever sang 'Love Machine' by Girls Aloud
FYD sang 'Beggin' by Madcon
Husstle sang 'Tainted Love' by Soft Cell
Princes and Rogues sang 'Video Killed
The Radio Star' by The Buggles
The Reason sang 'If You're Not The One'
by Daniel Bedingfield
Twem sang 'When Love Takes Over' by Kelly Rowland

One Direction hadn't been one of the groups that Simon had thought would definitely make *The X Factor* live shows but after their performance at Judges' Houses they had proved that they were real contenders. Other groups who Simon had thought would excel at this stage failed to make an impact, something that made choosing his top three really difficult.

After they were called by the production team and told to go and see Simon the boys were close to tears because they knew they were about to find out their fate and whether all the hard work they had put in had been worth it. As they lined up in front of Simon, Zayn had his arms around Liam and Louis; all five boys connected to each other for support. Simon said: 'My head is saying it's a risk and my heart is saying that you deserve a shot. And that's why it's been difficult... So I've made a decision... Guys, I've gone with my heart – you're through!'

The boys shouted 'Yes!' in excitement and then had a massive group hug. Harry ran over to hug Simon, closely followed by Niall and Zayn. To see their reaction take a look on YouTube – Zayn looks so happy. Louis, Niall and Harry all had tears in their eyes – they were so overcome with emotion. Simon told the boys: 'I am so impressed with all of you, I mean that.'

Zayn couldn't wait to ring his family and tell them the good news – he was going to be singing on live TV every Saturday night!

DID YOU KNOW?

While in Marbella, Zayn and Louis sneaked off together even though this wasn't allowed. They got some pizza and chatted on the beach. For Zayn, it was the perfect first trip abroad!

CHAPTER FOUR

SINGING TO
MILLIONS

The boys all lived at home with their families at this point but on their return to the UK, they had to get ready to move into the *X Factor* house in London. It would be their new home for as long as they were in the competition. Zayn was excited but it was daunting saying goodbye to his family and friends in Bradford. He would only get to see them at weekends when they came to see the live shows, and he was going to be so busy rehearsing all the time.

The first night Zayn and the other boys moved into the *X Factor* house all the contestants decided to have a sing-song together to celebrate being there and getting to the live shows. For the first week they could all relax because the productions hadn't yet started but, once they did, the aspiring pop stars would have to be prepared to say goodbye to a solo artist or group every week. Sunday nights became difficult as the singer voted off had to come back, pack their bags and leave, but, countering the sadness, Zayn and the boys were happy that they had made it through to another week.

DID YOU KNOW?

Zayn supports Manchester United football team, just like Harry and Louis. In an interview with *This Morning* Zayn was asked: 'if you could be one of the other guys in One Direction who would you choose?' He replied: 'I'd be Louis because I can't play football very well and he's a good footballer.'

The *X Factor* house was loud in the beginning because there were so many people living there but as the weeks went by, things quietened down. Zayn, Harry, Niall, Liam and Louis had all been given one small room to share but as people left, other bedrooms became available, so Zayn and Liam decided to move out and share another room. They hadn't fallen out with the others, it was just easier because every week they all gained more extra stuff and the room was so full of things, meaning it was hard to move around without tripping over something. Zayn and Liam were also able to keep their room a lot cleaner and tidier!

During *The X Factor* Zayn and the boys had to spend up to 18 hours a day rehearsing to get the harmonies right and to make sure that their performances were the best they could be. But they were never complacent; every week they thought they might be the ones going home. It is much harder being part of a group than being a solo artist. They were determined that they would share the lead singer responsibilities because all five were talented singers and they wanted to show people what each of them could do.

On a couple of occasions some people watching the show on television criticised their performances and suggested that the boys mimed rather than sang live. This hurt the boys because every single performance they did as a group was live. The only time that they mimed was during the Sunday night show, when all the contestants performed one song together. All the wannabe pop stars had to mime during that performance because they only had limited time to rehearse and all the songs were very high energy and involved a lot of movement. The general public couldn't vote after the group performances so these didn't impact on the final results.

The first time One Direction were accused of miming was in Week 5 – American Anthems week. During their performance of 'Kids In America' by Kim Wilde the camera focused in on Zayn and to some people it looked like he had missed his cue, even though you could still hear him sing. It wasn't actually Zayn's voice that you could hear, but Harry's, as he was singing at the time but because the camera was focused on Zayn, it made it look like Zayn was miming. That night poor Zayn was criticised a lot on Twitter and in the press.

RoseGardenAcs tweeted: 'One Direction miming the chorus. I'd send them straight to the naughty step.'

Alexander McNeil thought they were miming, too: 'Zayn REALLY dropped the ball on The #xfactor tonight… so obviously One Direction were miming parts… ARGH!'

The boys had given an amazing performance and should have been praised, not criticised. An *X Factor* spokesperson told the *Daily Mail*: 'All Saturday night competitive performances are performed and sung live by the contestants.

'And we'd take it very seriously if there were any suggestion otherwise.'

The judges had been impressed by their performance, with Louis Walsh saying: 'What a brilliant way to end the show! Listen, everywhere I go there's hysteria, it's building on this band. You remind me a bit of Westlife, Take That, Boyzone... you could be the next big band. I loved everything about the performance.'

Cheryl Cole commented: 'That absolutely cheered me up and brightened up my night; I thoroughly enjoyed that performance! You are great kids – I love chatting to you backstage. You are just good lads, nice lads. Great performance, good song choice!'

ONE DIRECTION'S *X FACTOR* PERFORMANCES

Week 1 – No. 1s – 'Viva La Vida' by Coldplay

Week 2 – Heroes – 'My Life Would Suck Without You' by Kelly Clarkson

Week 3 – Guilty Pleasures – 'Nobody Knows' by Pink

Week 4 – Halloween – 'Total Eclipse Of The Heart' by Bonnie Tyler

Week 5 – American Anthems – 'Kids In America' by Kim Wilde

Week 6 – Elton John – 'Something About The Way You Look Tonight'

Week 7 – Beatles – 'All You Need Is Love'

Week 8 – Rock – 'Summer Of '69' by Bryan Adams and 'You Are So Beautiful' by Joe Cocker

Week 9 – Semi Final – 'Only Girl In The World' by Rihanna and 'Chasing Cars' by Snow Patrol

Week 10 – Final – 'Your Song' by Elton John, 'She's the One' by Robbie Williams and 'Torn' by Natalie Imbruglia

Zayn loved performing on stage every weekend, singing with his new friends. Every Sunday when Dermot O'Leary announced who was safe and who was in the bottom two he felt a mixture of emotions – waiting for him to say that One Direction were through was torture. Every time he did, Zayn would hug the others and Simon – the boys couldn't help but jump up and down with relief and happiness.

Not everything about Zayn's *X Factor* journey was good, though. His grandad died a few days before the semi-final and Zayn was left heartbroken. He rushed home to Bradford to be with his family but made it back for the live show on the Saturday night. Zayn's grandad had been so proud of how well Zayn and the boys had been doing on the show. At the funeral the boys' version of 'You Are So Beautiful' was played – it was Zayn's grandad's favourite song.

All of the *X Factor* judges were so supportive of the boys, even though, for some, they were competing against their own acts.

In Week 3, after the boys had sung 'Nobody Knows' by Pink, Cheryl Cole said: 'You are my guilty pleasure. When you watch the TV and you see all the hysteria you caused when you went out there this week, that's what you should do. That's what boy bands should be about. Whenever The Beatles went anywhere they caused that level of hysteria. You're finding your feet now, I'm looking forward to seeing you improve even more.'

The next week they sang 'Total Eclipse Of The Heart' by Bonnie Tyler. Simon was really impressed, saying, 'Once again, a great performance! What I really admire about you guys is… I know people are under pressure when you go into a competition like this. You've got to remember you're 16, 17 years old, the way that you've conducted yourselves: don't

29

believe the hype, work hard, rehearse… Honestly, total pleasure working with you lot.'

After their performance of 'Something About The Way You Look Tonight' in Week 6, Dannii Minogue said: 'Guys, you are so consistent, it's scary! That song could have been really boring, but it was great – that's what I would love to hear you sing at your concerts, which I'm sure you will be doing one day [crowd cheers].'

Simon Cowell then told the boys and everyone watching at home: 'This is the first time in all the years of *X Factor* where I genuinely believe a group are going to win this competition. And you know what? I want to say this, what was so impressive, you've seen the girls and anything else you've remained focused, you've been really nice to the crew, you're nice to the fans and most importantly, everything that happened tonight from the choice of song to what they wore, it was all down to you. Guys, congratulations!'

During an interview the boys did for the *X Factor* website Liam said: 'Being on stage is absolutely amazing! I mean, we only spend such a short time on it but we love absolutely every second of it. We wouldn't change any of it, it's great!'

Zayn added: 'This for us is just unbelievable! We were all sat in the car today and I think it was Liam that said, "It feels like a dream and that we're all going to wake up, and our mums are gonna be like, *Wake up, get ready for school!* kind of thing."'

DID YOU KNOW?

Zayn was the *X Factor* contestant who spent the longest time in front of the mirror. Also, after Justin Bieber had appeared on one of the results shows, he offered to give Zayn dancing lessons.

It took nine weeks (and eleven amazing performances) for Zayn, Niall, Liam, Louis and Harry to make *The X Factor* final and compete for the recording deal on offer. Their rivals for the title of *X Factor* winners 2010 were Rebecca Ferguson, Cher Lloyd and Matt Cardle. In the days leading up to the final all the finalists got to enjoy a day in their respective hometowns, or in One Direction's case, a few hours in the hometowns of Harry, Louis, Zayn and Liam. Sadly for Niall they were unable to make the trip over to Ireland in case they got snowed in and couldn't fly back for the final.

The first thing they did was head to a TV studio to do a live link with Ireland AM so that One Direction's Irish fans wouldn't miss out, and then they travelled to Doncaster to visit Louis' old school. After a brief visit the boys jumped in their car and travelled to Holmes Chapel, Cheshire, where Harry is from (it was also where they got to know each other in the weeks before the Judges' Houses round). Zayn and the boys enjoyed a small party at Harry's family home before travelling to Zayn's hometown of Bradford. Rather than visit Zayn's school or the family home, they headed for the city centre and the HMV music store. Hundreds of people lined the street, all desperate to see Zayn. He couldn't get over the reception – only a few months earlier he'd been able to walk down the street unrecognised. Zayn admitted to the others that he would love to do an album-signing in the store one day. Before long, the boys needed to be on the move again as they had a show to put on in Liam's hometown of Wolverhampton. They met Simon there and performed three songs for the fans who had come out to show their support.

The boys were so tired that night once they got back to the *X Factor* house and crawled into their beds. They had clocked up so many miles but Zayn and the others thought it had been so worth it just to see the smiles on the faces of the fans in Bradford, Doncaster, Holmes Chapel and Wolverhampton. Now they just needed to rest as much as they could until the Saturday night and then if they got through, think about the Sunday night. They were about to have the busiest weekend of their lives so far.

SATURDAY – WHO SANG WHAT? – SONG 1:

One Direction – 'Your Song' by Elton John
Cher Lloyd – Mash up of '369' by Cupid Ft B.o.B and 'Get Your Freak On' by Missy Elliott
Matt Cardle – 'Here With Me' by Dido
Rebecca Ferguson – 'Like A Star' by Corinne Bailey Rae

WHAT THE JUDGES THOUGHT OF ONE DIRECTION'S PERFORMANCE:

Louis Walsh: 'Hey, One Direction, you're in the final! I hope you're here tomorrow night. It's amazing how five guys have gelled so well. I know you're all best friends. I've never seen a band cause so much hysteria so early in their career – I definitely think that you've got an amazing future. Niall, everybody in Ireland must vote for Niall, yes!'

Dannii Minogue: 'Guys, you have worked so hard in this competition. You were thrown together, you deserve to be here and I'd love to see you in the final tomorrow.'

Cheryl Cole: 'You know what? I have thoroughly enjoyed watching you guys growing every week, having the most amount of fun possible, and I think that you deserve to be standing on that stage tomorrow night.'

Simon Cowell: 'I just would like to say after hearing the first two performances tonight – Matt and Rebecca – they were so good, my heart was sinking. And then you came up on stage... You've got to remember that you're sixteen, seventeen years old, and each of you proved that you should be there as individual singers – you gave it 1,000 per cent. It's been an absolute pleasure working with you. I really hope people bother to pick up the phone, put you through to tomorrow, because you deserve to be there.'

SATURDAY – WHO SANG WHAT? – SONG 2 – THE DUETS:

One Direction – 'She's The One' with Robbie Williams
Cher Lloyd – Mash up of 'Where Is The Love' and 'I Gotta Feeling' with Will.i.am
Matt Cardle – 'Unfaithful' with Rihanna
Rebecca Ferguson – 'Beautiful' with Christina Aguilera

WHAT THE BOYS THOUGHT:

Zayn loved singing with Robbie Williams in the final because he'd spent time getting to know them during the day – he didn't just show up at the last minute to sing. For Louis and Niall it was a dream come true because they are huge Robbie Williams' fans.

For the duet the boys wore brightly coloured suits and stood with Liam on the left, then Niall, Harry in the middle, then Louis with Zayn on the right-hand side. Zayn's suit was green and he wore a black shirt – he looked absolutely gorgeous. Liam started the singing and then Harry took over before Zayn, Niall and Louis joined in with 'She's the one'. Their harmonies were perfect. The audience must have been wondering where Robbie was, but he appeared as soon as Louis said: 'Right, there's a man who is a hero to all of us. Here he is, the incredible Robbie Williams!'

Robbie joined the line, standing between Harry and Louis. Zayn might have not been into Robbie's music that much before but he was so happy as they sang together – he was bopping along to the music in between his singing parts. Robbie high-fived them all and at the end of their performance they had a group hug.

The boys were so grateful that Robbie had been willing to sing with them and Simon thanked him personally, saying: 'Robbie is a great friend to the show – very, very generous with his time and he's made these boys' night of their lives! Thank you, Robbie.'

THE RESULT:

Every result show had been very tense but it was even more nerve-wracking for Zayn as he waited with the boys and Simon to find out if they had done enough to make Sunday's final show or whether they would be going home in fourth place. The first name that Dermot called out was Rebecca Ferguson – she was the first act safe. Next, he called One Direction and Zayn couldn't believe it. After jumping up and down, the boys hugged Simon – they were so excited! The final act joining them was Matt Cardle, which meant that Cher Lloyd had reached the end of the road and would be leaving that night.

DID YOU KNOW?

Zayn reckons one day One Direction would be great guest judges on the UK series of *The X Factor*. He told 110% Pop: 'I'm sure we would be very interesting to watch, actually. We haven't been approached for that yet. If we do get approached, I'm sure we'll try and sort out that we're all sitting in one chair, yeah.'

SINGING TO MILLIONS

SUNDAY – WHO SANG WHAT?

One Direction sang 'Torn' by Natalie Imbruglia
Matt Cardle sang 'Firework' by Katy Perry
Rebecca Ferguson sang 'Sweet Dreams' by Eurythmics

WHAT THE JUDGES THOUGHT OF ONE DIRECTION'S PERFORMANCE:

Louis Walsh: 'One Direction, you're in the final! You could be the first band to win *The X Factor* – it's up to the public at home. But you've got brilliant chemistry, I love the harmonies, I love the song choice and we've got five new pop stars!'

Dannii Minogue: 'Guys, you've done all the right things to make your place here in the final. That was a fantastic performance! Whatever happens tonight, I'm sure you guys are going to go on and release records and be the next big band.'

Cheryl Cole: 'It's been so lovely to watch you guys from your first audition – to think that was only a few months ago. I really believe that you've got a massive future ahead of you and I wanna say thank you for being such lovely guys to be around. It's been great getting to know you and good luck with the show tonight.'

Simon Cowell: 'Let's be clear, anyone who comes into this final has got a great chance of bettering their future. But this is a competition and in terms of the competition, in terms of who's worked the hardest, who I think deserves to win based on the future of something we haven't seen before, I would love to hear your names read out at the end of the competition. Because I think you deserve it.'

ZAYN MALIK

THE RESULT:

There were two results on the Sunday night: the first to find out who had come third and the second to announce who had won *The X Factor 2010*. Waiting for the results on the Saturday night had been intense but time seemed to stand still for the first results of the Sunday show. The first name Dermot O'Leary called was Matt Cardle so it was either One Direction or Rebecca Ferguson who had finished in third place. Sadly for Zayn, Harry, Niall, Liam and Louis, it was Rebecca who was named as the second act to go through to the last part of the show: they had finished in third place.

Their mentor Simon was gutted and turned his back straight away, hiding his face from the cameras. Zayn and the boys were devastated, trying their best not to cry. They had come so close. As they went over to congratulate Rebecca, Zayn was slightly behind the others – he was so upset. They watched the video montage of their *X Factor* journey before host Dermot asked what the highlight had been for them. Louis said: 'It's been absolutely incredible. For me, the highlight was when we first sang together at Judges' Houses, that was unbelievable and you know what? We've done our absolute best, we've worked hard.'

Zayn added: 'We're definitely going to stay together – this isn't the last of One Direction!'

Simon agreed with Zayn, saying: 'I'm absolutely gutted for them, but look, for everyone who has bothered to pick up the phone over the past few weeks, I really appreciate it and all I can say is this is just the beginning!'

Zayn, Niall, Liam, Louis and Harry had to leave the stage with Simon as Matt and Rebecca had one more song each to sing. The two remaining contestants had to sing the song they would release, should they win – it must have been hard on the boys because they had prepared a song too, but they didn't get the opportunity to sing it.

Later on in the show Dermot announced that Matt was the winner and Rebecca was runner-up. The boys were happy for Matt because they had become close to him during their *X Factor* journey. All along they had said that if they didn't win, they wanted Matt to do so.

After the show, the boys tweeted from their official Twitter account: 'Congratulations Matt! Please support Matt by buying When We Collide... iTunes.'

Even though the boys were gutted they didn't win, they soon had something to smile about: Simon offered them a record deal. He told them to meet him in his office and the next day offered them a £2 million recording contract with his company, Syco. *X Factor* winner Matt Cardle had secured a £1 million recording contract so the boys actually did better by not winning! They were sworn to secrecy because Simon didn't want the news getting out straightaway – it wouldn't have been fair on Matt or the other *X Factor* acts who hadn't yet secured deals.

Zayn told *The X Factor Australia*: 'When we got to the final, we were like, we want to win this... we got kicked out, we came third. At the time we were massively disappointed.

'The next day Simon called us into the Sony offices and we signed a contract so that was crazy!'

DID YOU KNOW?

Simon Cowell isn't as scary as he is often portrayed. Zayn described what he was like as a mentor to New Zealand radio hosts Jay-Jay, Mike and Dom. He said: 'He was very different to what we thought he was going to be like because obviously he gets portrayed as this massively scary figure who's like, the head of the music industry, and we met him and he's such a cool, down-to-earth guy… You can talk to him about football, girls and he's really cool, and he's stayed completely faithful to us. He took full control of the One Direction campaign and everything. He's still there and he's still making decisions.'

DID YOU KNOW?

In taking part in *The X Factor* the boys had the opportunity to meet lots of singers and bands, including JLS, The Wanted, Westlife and Take That. Zayn and his bandmates were able to see how other boy bands work and play together.

Here is a list of the acts that performed as part of the results shows:

Week 1 – Joe McElderry and Usher
Week 2 – Diana Vickers and Katy Perry
Week 3 – Cheryl Cole and Michael Bublé
Week 4 – Jamiroquai and Rihanna
Week 5 – Shayne Ward and Kylie Minogue
Week 6 – JLS, Westlife and Take That
Week 7 – Olly Murs
Week 8 – The Wanted, Justin Bieber and Nicole Scherzinger
Week 9 – Alexandra Burke, the cast of *Glee* and the Black Eyed Peas
Week 10 – Rihanna and Christina Aguilera

In Week 6 Liam told the official *X Factor* website: 'It's great to have all the boy bands coming on the show and we have a lot of questions we want to ask them because they are doing what we want to do. We're looking forward to seeing all of them, but Niall is really excited about Westlife!' Niall wanted to meet Gary Barlow too and Louis was looking forward to seeing Robbie Williams.

Our favourite boys might not have entered *The X Factor* as a group but they have always admired boy bands. If they had to pick a favourite, Liam and Zayn would go for N Sync, Harry would pick Take That and Westlife would get Niall's vote, 'because they're Irish.' Louis doesn't seem to have a favourite but he is a big Robbie Williams' fan so maybe Take That with Robbie.

All the boy bands who have met One Direction on *The X Factor* were full of praise for Liam, Niall, Harry, Zayn and Louis. Of course they might end up fighting them in the charts one day but for now they can just be friends. Shane Filan from Westlife told *X* magazine: 'They're the whole package. They're good singers, they're good-looking lads and they're quite cool. They're like a band full of Justin Biebers and they've got everything the girls will love.'

After the show finished Zayn went home for Christmas and enjoyed spoiling his family with lots of presents. He bought Doniya a pair of Ugg boots – she had wanted them for ages but they had been out of her price range. For New Year's Eve he partied with his friends. It was nice to be plain old Zayn again and not Zayn from *The X Factor*. But he could only stay in Bradford for a short time – he had to move permanently to London, something that was hard for both Zayn and his family. Mum Trisha would have liked nothing more than for him to move back home into his old bedroom but at the same time she was delighted that he was living his dream.

CHAPTER FIVE

UP ALL NIGHT

2011 was a huge year for Zayn, Harry, Niall, Liam and Louis, and they were really busy from the very start. First, they had the *X Factor* tour to look forward to, which went to the major arenas around the UK and Ireland, and then they had to work on their debut album, *Up All Night*.

Before tour rehearsals started, the boys had to get their passports out again and fly to Los Angeles to start choosing songs and recording with legendary record producer RedOne. Zayn was overwhelmed that they were given the opportunity to work with RedOne (real name Nadir Khayat) because he had worked with Michael Jackson on his final album, *Invincible*, and had also collaborated with huge stars like Lady Gaga, Nicole Scherzinger, Backstreet Boys and Cher. Zayn believes RedOne helped give an anthemic vibe to *Up All Night*. He told the *Daily Star*: 'To work with RedOne was such a big deal. It's more like the sound he created with Nicole Scherzinger. Powerful.'

Simon didn't want to keep the fans waiting too long for the album and the boys were eager to start recording tracks too. Zayn loved how warm it was in America – it had been really cold in the run-up to Christmas in the UK so it was nice to be back wearing T-shirts and shorts again. The boys didn't have that much time to sunbathe and enjoy the sights as their schedules were pretty tightly packed but Zayn still managed to fit in a few shopping trips. He loves high-topped trainers so picked up a nice pair of black Nike ones as a treat. Back then the boys could walk around Los Angeles without being recognised but there is no way they could do that today – they'd get mobbed!

DID YOU KNOW?

Looking good matters to Zayn and he loves being fashionable. He topped MyCelebrityFashion.co.uk's list of the Best Dressed Celebrity Males of 2013. Previously, the title had been held by Harry in 2012 but this time he dropped to fourth in the 2013 list. In second place was radio DJ Nick Grimshaw, in third place was David Beckham and in fifth place came Chris Brown.

The boys were only in Los Angeles for a few days and then they had to fly back to the UK so that they could attend rehearsals for the tour. It was going to be a new experience for them, singing to up to 20,000 people each night. Zayn's family couldn't wait to go and see the guys perform. Meanwhile the boys had to learn how to fill the stage and perform some dance moves during their songs, so there was a lot to take in. They weren't too apprehensive, though, because the other X *Factor* acts had to learn everything from scratch too, and it would be cool to hang out with them, especially since they hadn't seen many of them since the *X Factor* wrap party.

Zayn, Niall, Liam, Louis and Harry performed five songs during each concert: 'Only Girl', 'Chasing Cars', 'Kids In America', 'My Life Would Suck Without You' and a song called 'Forever Young' by 80s synth-pop group Alphaville, which would have been their first single, had they won *The X Factor*. The first show was at Birmingham's LG Arena on 19 February and the finale would take place at Cardiff's CIA on 9 April 2011.

Once the tour was over, Zayn and the boys had to say goodbye to many of the acts as those who hadn't managed to secure a recording deal would have to go back to their normal lives. But Zayn, Liam, Harry, Niall and Louis wouldn't have many opportunities to socialise with the people who were staying on in London because they were going to be so busy.

Zayn had loved being on the tour but getting back in the recording studio was even better. He learnt so much from the amazing songwriters and record producers they were working with and the boys had a blast, tucking into takeaways and messing around when they could. They had to work hard but they were allowed to enjoy themselves too.

DID YOU KNOW?

If Zayn ever has an argument with any of the boys, he buys them all a takeaway to make up for it!

Because of his love of English from a young age Zayn has also been interested in poetry and felt that the songs they were writing were like poems set to music. He loved having the opportunity to co-write songs and put his own stamp on them.

The boys flew out to Los Angeles again and they also spent time recording in Sweden.

During their time on *The X Factor* the boys had received vocal training from Savan Kotecha, one of the best vocal coaches in the world. Savan is also a talented songwriter and has written songs for Britney Spears, Leona Lewis, Westlife, Usher and many more international stars. After *The X Factor* finished, he was asked whether he would be interested in writing songs for One Direction – he jumped at the chance. He had loved working with Zayn, Harry, Niall, Liam and Louis – he found them full of energy and eager to learn. During *The X Factor*, he had written a funny song for them called 'Vas Happenin' Boys'. In it, he sings about Harry being a slob and needing to win *The X Factor* because he can't get a job and says that Harry's dad could be Mick Jagger. He also sings that Zayn is the master of echoes, Louis needs a boat, Niall was raised by leprechauns and Liam looks sad when he sings. To hear the song for yourself, check it out on YouTube – Savan and the boys had lots of fun filming it.

On the boys' first album, *Up All Night*, Savan co-wrote 'What Makes You Beautiful', 'I Wish', 'One Thing', 'Na Na Na', 'Up All Night' and 'Save You Tonight'. Other songwriters and producers who worked on the album included award-winning producer and songwriter Steve Robson, who has worked with Take That, Faith Hill, James Martin, Olly Murs, Leona Lewis and many more world-class performers. Steve co-wrote 'Everything About You' and 'Same Mistakes' with songwriter Wayne Hector. Wayne has written songs for Nicki Minaj, The Wanted and Westlife, and has had over 30 No. 1 hits – quite an achievement. The producer of Britney Spears's '… Baby One More Time', Rami Yacoub, also worked on the boys' album, co-writing 'What Makes You Beautiful', 'I Wish' and 'One Thing' with Savan and Carl Falk (Carl co-wrote the record-breaking 'Starships' for Nicki Minaj).

Out of the 15 tracks on *Up All Night* (13 on the standard version, plus the two tracks on the Limited Edition Yearbook version of the album) Zayn's favourite has to be 'Tell Me A Lie', which was written by Kelly Clarkson. If he had to sum up the album in one word, he would pick 'anthemic'.

DID YOU KNOW?

On the album Zayn has approximately five-and-a-half minutes of solos.

Zayn was so excited when he could walk into any record store in the UK and buy *Up All Night*! It was released in Ireland on 18 November 2011 and three days later in the UK. His family and friends were all so proud of him and rushed out to buy multiple copies. To have it charted at No. 1 in Ireland was a dream come true for the boys (especially Niall). It charted at No. 2 in the UK after 138,163 copies were sold in the first week of its release and it did even better worldwide when released in 2012. It was released in America on 13 March 2013 and ended up being No. 1 in America after 176,000 copies were sold in the first week. One Direction were the first UK/Ireland group to get to No. 1 in America with their debut album. *Up All Night* was also No. 1 in Australia, Canada, Croatia, Italy, Mexico, New Zealand and Sweden.

Zayn's former teachers were so proud of him when they heard that *Up All Night* had reached No. 1 in America. John Edwards, head teacher of Lower Fields Primary, told the *Telegraph & Angus*: 'It's brilliant. The thing that impresses me about Zayn is that fame hasn't changed him one bit. He pops into school every so often. He is totally unaffected, respectful, a delightful young man. It couldn't have happened to a nicer person.

'We followed him closely through the competition [*The X Factor*] and we were delighted when they were so successful, but never envisaged it would become a worldwide phenomenon.'

The head teacher of Zayn's high school, Steve Curran, also told the newspaper: 'We are delighted and proud of Zayn's success and would like to congratulate One Direction on their US success.

'We would like to pass on our best wishes from all staff and students of Tong High School.'

The first single the boys released was 'What Makes You Beautiful' – a far better choice than doing a cover of 'Forever Young', which would have been their first single had they won *The X Factor*. It was No. 1 on iTunes within 15 minutes of being released. 'What Makes You Beautiful' was also No. 1 in America, Ireland, Mexico and the UK. A big hit worldwide, it ended up breaking lots of records, topping charts and going multi-platinum in many countries.

They filmed the video for 'What Makes You Beautiful' in July 2011 on a beach in Malibu, California. It was directed by John Urbano, who would go on to direct a lot of the boys' future videos. It took them 18 hours the first day and 14 hours the next to film the 3 minutes 27 seconds of footage. Harry tried to sunbathe when the cameras weren't rolling, and on one occasion he fell asleep. Zayn sneaked up on him and decided to cover him in sand as a prank. Harry got a big surprise when he woke up and saw what Zayn had done!

The second single the boys released in the UK and Ireland was 'Gotta Be You' and it was released on 11 November 2011. The boys didn't have much chance to promote it though because they were really busy, but it still did well, charting at No. 3. They had only filmed the video a month before in Plattsburgh at the State University of New York and at Lake Placid, New York. The story behind the video is that the boys are leaving school and making their way to the lake to have a bonfire with some female friends. At the end of the video there is a fireworks display and Zayn walks towards a girl and kisses her.

Filming was eventful for the boys. Louis burnt out the cooling system on the Mini Cooper he had to drive, Zayn crashed his moped and they all ended up going for a swim in the lake. They had found a small boat and decided to go out on the lake together, but Louis decided to have a laugh and throw Liam overboard. The other lads didn't want him to do it to them so they started wrestling, which caused the boat to capsize. They had to swim back to shore and were told off for being silly.

Zayn chatted to *Celebs on Sunday* magazine about what happened with the moped. He confided: 'I smashed up a Vespa… I'm making this sound more glamorous than it actually was. It just span out and went crazy, ran on about two metres and hit some gravel. And it was a limited edition, worth thousands. They had to put red nail polish on it to cover the scratches.'

Liam added: 'He'd never driven a moped before and he had this brand new red one we were using in a video shoot – and crashed it.'

The boys' second single to be released worldwide (and third release in the UK and Ireland) was 'One Thing'. For this video they decided to stay in the UK and filmed in London as they travelled in an open-topped double-decker bus. Lots of fans turned up at Trafalgar Square to be part of the video after the boys tweeted to invite them and the boys were really grateful.

They filmed it on 28 November 2011, only weeks after they'd filmed the video for 'Gotta Be You' in America but there was quite a gap before it was available to buy – it was available for digital download on 6 January 2012 in Austria, Denmark, Estonia, France, Germany, Greece, Hungary, Italy, Latvia, New Zealand, Poland, Portugal, Spain and Switzerland. On 13 February 2012, it was released in the UK and in America on 22 May 2012. It was No. 3 in Australia, No. 4 in Hungary, No. 6 in Ireland, No. 9 in the UK and No. 39 in America.

Their final release from *Up All Night* was 'More Than This', which was released in Australia, Ireland and the UK. The single's video was simply a recording of the boys performing the song and it premiered in Australia. Released for digital download in Australia on 25 May 2012 and released in the UK and Ireland on 26 June 2012, it did best in Ireland, charting at No. 39. It was No. 49 in the Australian charts and No. 86 in the UK charts.

UP ALL NIGHT – TRACK BY TRACK

Track 1 – 'What Makes You Beautiful' – was written by Rami Yacoub, Carl Falk and Savan Kotecha. It was produced by Rami Yacoub and Carl Falk.

Track 2 – 'Gotta Be You' – was written by Steve Mac and August Rigo. It was produced by Steve Mac.

Track 3 – 'One Thing' – was written by Rami Yacoub, Carl Falk and Savan Kotecha. It was produced by Rami Yacoub and Carl Falk.

Track 4 – 'More Than This' – was written by Jamie Scott. It was produced by Brian Rawling and Paul Meehan.

Track 5 – 'Up All Night' – was written by Savan Kotecha and Matt Squire. It was produced by Matt Squire.

Track 6 – 'I Wish' – was written by Rami Yacoub, Carl

Falk and Savan Kotecha. It was produced by Rami Yacoub and Carl Falk.

Track 7 – 'Tell Me a Lie' – was written by Kelly Clarkson, Tom Meredith and Shep Solomon. It was produced by Tom Meredith and Shep Solomon.

Track 8 – 'Taken' – was written by Toby Gad, Lindy Robbins and 1D. It was produced by Toby Gad.

Track 9 – 'I Want' – was written by Tom Fletcher. It was produced by Richard Stannard and Ash Howes.

Track 10 – 'Everything About You' – was written by Steven Robson, Wayne Hector and 1D. It was produced by Steven Robson.

Track 11 – 'Same Mistakes' – was written by Steven Robson, Wayne Hector and 1D. It was produced by Steven Robson.

Track 12 – 'Save You Tonight' – was written by RedOne, BeatGeek, Jimmy Joker, Teddy Sky, Achraf Jannusi, Alaina Beaton and Savan Kotecha. It was produced by RedOne, BeatGeek and Jimmy Joker.

Track 13 – 'Stole My Heart' – was written by Jamie Scott and Paul Meehan. It was produced by Brian Rawling and Paul Meehan.

Track 14 – 'Stand Up' – was written by Roy Stride and Josh Wilkinson. It was produced by Richard Stannard.

Track 15 – 'Moments' – was written by Ed Sheeran and Si Hulbert. It was produced by Si Hulbert.

WHAT THE REVIEWERS THOUGHT:

In *Billboard*'s review of the album, Jason Lipshutz wrote: 'Let's get this right out of the way: first single "What Makes You Beautiful" is the real deal. The song may not have earned its win over Adele's "Someone Like You" at the BRIT Awards, but

One Direction's smash hit is as endlessly playable as "Bye Bye Bye" or "Everybody (*Backstreet's Back*)", and as unstoppable as its 65 million Vevo views suggest. As the first song on *Up All Night*, "What Makes You Beautiful" leads a front-loaded effort – its first three songs have doubled as its first three singles in the U.K. – that can make the debut album feel a bit top-heavy. Themes of innocent romance are constant throughout *Up All Night*, but tracks like "Gotta Be You" and "More Than This" hit a mark more smoothly than songs like "Everything About You" and "Taken".

'Even on its weakest tracks, however, *Up All Night* demonstrates an originality in sound that was necessary for the revitalization of the boy band movement.'

Hollywood Life were equally impressed, giving the album 4 out of 5 stars. They stated in their review: 'Not since the golden age of boy bands in the mid-'90s has a group emerged to convince me that the classic formula can still work – that is, until One Direction entered the picture. The British-Irish fivesome's debut album, *Up All Night*, is already burning up the U.S. charts, and is it any wonder why?

'With catchy melodies, thoughtful lyrics, and more energy than a thousand Justin Bieber fans in a tiny box, *Up All Night* feels like summer and Christmas and my birthday all rolled into one. In short, it just makes us happy.'

The *Digital Spy* reviewer Robert Copsey thought 1D delivered just what their fans wanted, writing: 'Lead single "What Makes You Beautiful" – a toe-tapping, Pink-meets-McFly mash up with a breezy guitar pop melody – sets the tone to a tee; with the lion's share of uptempos, including "One Thing" and the title track, following a similar template. Fortunately, there's too much enthusiasm to accuse them of negligence.

'More surprising is their ability to carry off a sizeable ballad. The earworm chorus on "More Than This" and heartfelt lyrics on "Taken" ("You don't really want my heart/ You just like to know you can") are some of the best slowies to come out of boyband land in recent years; making their decision to release the significantly less exciting "Gotta Be You" as the second cut all the more mind-boggling. Sure, it's only playground love, but sometimes that's the best kind.'

In February 2013 'What Makes You Beautiful' was certified quadruple platinum by the Recording Industry of America (RIAA) after selling 4 million copies. For Zayn, getting to No. 1 in America was beyond what he had ever hoped for. He would have been happy if One Direction were just popular in the UK, and to have hit singles in America and around the world was unbelievable.

DID YOU KNOW?

Billboard's 21 under 21 list saw Justin Bieber as the most powerful young music star in the world, and One Direction in second place. What an achievement!

McFly's lead singer Tom Fletcher wrote the ninth track on the album, 'I Want'. He had originally written the song for his sister Carrie but decided to give it to Zayn and the boys to record for the album. He enjoyed working with One Direction, telling the *Daily Star*: 'They're a really likeable bunch of guys and they've got everything it takes to hit the big time.' He enjoyed writing songs with them, as did his McFly bandmates Danny Jones and Dougie Poynter. They worked hard but played hard too, playing FIFA football games and messing around.

Ed Sheeran wrote the track 'Moments', which was one of

the boys' favourite songs from the album. He had actually
written it many years before but realised it was more suited to
a group rather than the type of track he should record himself.
Ed explained to News.com how it ended up on *Up All Night*:
'I had a CD of 40 songs I was giving to publishers. Harry was
staying at my guitarist's friend's house at the time. They were
putting their album together and they didn't have enough
songs. I said, "Here's a CD. If you want one of these songs, have
it." And it got on the album. It was a song I was never going to
use. To have it on a multi-platinum selling album is quite nice.'

The songs Zayn finds hardest to sing on the album are 'Save
You Tonight' and 'Tell Me A Lie' because he has to sing high.

DID YOU KNOW?

In July 2012 Zayn treated himself to a Bentley
Continental GT car costing a massive £32,000 ($48,681
dollars). Footballer David Beckham and rapper Nicki
Minaj have the same car. It might seem to be very
expensive to fans but it is a third of the price of Harry's
Audi R8 Coupe.

CHAPTER SIX

FINDING HOME

When Zayn first left the *X Factor* house he moved with the other boys into a hotel but after returning to London after the Christmas break, they were transferred to a luxury apartment, paid for by their record company. All five of them lived together in the beginning but after a while Harry and Louis shared one apartment and the others had an apartment each.

The apartment complex was in Friern Barnet, North London. It used to be Colney Hatch Lunatic Asylum in the Victorian era and was a hospital for mental patients until 1993. It was converted into luxury apartments which now cost from £500,000 to buy. Former and current residents include Girls Aloud, JLS, The Wanted, The Saturdays, Tulisa Contostavlos and England footballers Ashley Cole and Jermaine Pennant. The complex has a tennis court, gym, swimming pool and great security to prevent any fans from trying to sneak inside the gated community.

From 2012 the boys started moving out and buying their own houses in London. Zayn chose a £2 million ($3.2 million) five-bedroomed house. Zayn's house is really close to a house that Harry bought for £3 million ($4.8 million). Harry also owns a house in East London.

Before he moved in, Zayn told the *Sun*: 'I have no furniture to fill the house but I'll give it a good go.

'It's really nice for me because growing up, we never really owned our own house – we always lived in a rented property. I don't come from a lot of money so for me to have my own house is a big achievement. That's all I ever wanted to do.'

DID YOU KNOW?

Niall thinks that Zayn is the moodiest member of 1D and is great at doing impressions. Also, if Zayn wasn't a singer, he would like to be an actor. Before *The X Factor* he thought he would go to university to study English and become an English teacher.

A few weeks later *Now Magazine* reported: 'A team of removal men were spotted moving some of the 19-year-old One Direction singer's possessions into the property earlier this week. These included his blue motorcycle and two life-sized models, which bizarrely appeared to be of himself. One of the heavy mannequins was clad in a leather jacket and trilby hat while the other wore a white suit and one red glove. Zayn's new house boasts a number of impressive features, including a wine cellar, underfloor heating, a steam room, Jacuzzi and roof deck. The property's flat roof, large windows and unusual chrome doors give it a unique space-age look.'

The *Sun* reported that Zayn's new home had a panic room so that he could hide if anyone ever broke into his house. They said it was also fitted with bulletproof doors, high-tech monitors and reinforced walls.

Zayn didn't just want to have a nice house for himself, though: he wanted to treat his whole family so he bought them a luxury home in Bradford. He told *Parade* magazine: 'Now that we have a bit of money, it is nice to get gifts for people. Before I was getting and not really giving.'

The moment when his mum and sisters received the keys to their new home was shown in the trailer of the One Direction movie, *This Is Us*. Trisha was crying tears of happiness and called her 'sunshine' to tell him how grateful she is. She said: 'I know that you always used to say, "I'll get you a house one day when I'm older". But thank you for what you've done for us – I'm so proud of you.'

An emotional Zayn replied: 'Well, get off the phone then before I start crying.'

DID YOU KNOW?

Zayn is the member of 1D who struggles most with fame but he worries about Harry because he gets a hard time from the press and in forums. Zayn told the *Mirror*: 'He is the baby of the group but people seem to forget that because of the way that he is and that he is so charming.

'So it is a little bit upsetting sometimes if you see him with the weight of the world on his shoulders. It does annoy us a bit. He's a young kid and people are just giving him grief for no reason.'

CHAPTER SEVEN

GIRLS

Zayn says that he would love to be able to say that being a member of 1D hasn't made him more appealing to girls than he was before he joined the group but he can't, because it wouldn't be true. That said, he has always had admirers – it's just that now he has millions of them!

Zayn was eight when he wrote his first love letter. He can still remember the first girl he gave a Valentine's card to, but he won't reveal her name. There was a special Valentine's post box at his school so he posted his card in there and then it was delivered to her in class. He had his first kiss when he was nine or ten with a girl called Sophie Kirk. She was taller than Zayn and he couldn't reach so he needed to stand on a brick to be tall enough to lock lips with her. He thinks it was a bit like the Yellow Pages adverts. He didn't really like the kiss at all and found it embarrassing; he didn't want his family to find out he had kissed a girl either. He told *Heat* magazine: 'She was one of triplets and I kind of dated all three of them.'

DID YOU KNOW?
Zayn has a mole on one of his ribs.

Zayn started liking girls when he was in high school and had his first proper girlfriend when he was fifteen. They dated for nine months before splitting up. Zayn hasn't been out with many people and has only had about three serious relationships in his whole life. He says he never lies about his girlfriends or past relationships, telling *Top of the Pops* magazine: 'I've always been honest about that. What's the point of lying? You'll just get found out and then you'll look an idiot.'

When Zayn was at school he went through a phase where he wore a lot of hoodies and had a shaved head – he thought it made him look cool. Now he is in One Direction he likes having his hair longer and fans love his quiff. Every now and then though, he fancies having a change and in June 2012 he nearly decided to shave his hair off until fans on Twitter convinced him otherwise.

DID YOU KNOW?
Zayn's dad was his hairdresser when he was a child.

Zayn cares more about a girl's personality than her looks, although he admits he was quite shallow when he was younger. He likes intelligent girls, who have amazing smiles and he thinks you can tell a lot from a girl's eyes. He doesn't like girls who play mind games and prefers it when they are honest, as opposed to the types who say one thing and mean something else. His favourite chat-up line is 'What's happening?'

While living in the *X Factor* house the press linked Zayn to his fellow contestant Cher Lloyd because they were close in age and enjoyed spending time together. She decided to set the record straight and said in one of her video diaries: 'You asked if I was going out with Zayn... I'm not! He came in this morning in a green all-in-one... A green all-in-one! I don't think so, I really don't think so. Not cool!'

DID YOU KNOW?

An ideal date for Zayn would be going out for a meal, watching a movie at the cinema and then returning home to 'chill' with some drinks.

Once the competition was over, Zayn did end up dating one of the hopefuls, though. While they were taking part in the *X Factor* Live Tour he started to date Rebecca Ferguson, who had finished in second place. There was a six-year age gap and the press loved gossiping about them because Rebecca has two kids. Rebecca told the *Mirror*: 'I was with him for three months and people put so much focus on it because we were in the public eye.

'I was 24 then and I'd had two kids and other relationships so remember I'd had a lot of life experience before that. He's a footnote in my life maybe.'

Zayn told *new!* magazine: 'It shouldn't have happened. It was just a wrong idea from the start.

'It did end quite badly so we don't talk any more. We're not in touch at all.'

In April 2012, Zayn went public about his relationship with Perrie Edwards from the girl group Little Mix. They both tweeted after being on a cinema date. Perrie wrote: 'Just went to see avengers assemble and it was #boring. Good night though! xD @zaynmalik'

He replied: '@PerrieLittleMix yeah tonight was fun lets do it again sometime ;) x x'

DID YOU KNOW?

Before Zayn dated Perrie his celebrity crushes were Megan Fox and Jessica Alba.

Perrie's group Little Mix won *The X Factor* in 2011 after beating solo artists Marcus Collins and Amelia Lily. Zayn had admitted in an interview during the competition that he fancied Little Mix but he had no idea back then that he would end up dating one of them! It must be nice for Zayn that Perrie understands what it's like to be on *The X Factor* and having to deal with instant fame. Before they started dating, he asked if she was up to having a relationship in the spotlight, because girlfriends of the other boys had suffered abuse.

Only weeks after their first date some 1D fans began bombarding Perrie with vile Tweets and even threatening to kill her. It was really horrible and true 1D fans were horrified by what was going on. Perrie ended up having to delete her Twitter account for a while just to stop the messages; the whole situation left Zayn feeling very angry and upset.

Despite the hassle Perrie received on Twitter she continued to date Zayn and, in May 2012, told *This Morning*: 'Obviously we are together, and everyone knows that now. I'm really, really happy.' She is thankful that a lot of One Direction fans are also Little Mix fans, and believes that having to deal with horrible Tweets has just made herself and Zayn toughen up.

Throughout their relationship some girls have claimed that Zayn has asked for their number or cheated on Perrie with them, but Zayn insists what they say is all lies. They just want to make some money selling their stories and split Zayn and Perrie up. For a while Zayn ended up following Perrie's lead and deleted his Twitter account, telling followers: 'Don't worry about me, im fine. I just deleted my account because of all the hate i was getting just by tweeting something simple. And all the rumours of me smoking weed and cheating. I dont need to read any of that negativity.' He also said that he was sick of seeing his mum and Perrie being upset by the nasty comments. But the rumours didn't split Zayn and Perrie up and he helped her get over a bad bout of tonsillitis in December 2012. Perrie enjoys doing the same things as Zayn and admitted to *Look Magazine*: 'We just chill out on the sofa. I'll wear the purple onesie Zayn bought me – he's got one, too!

'Everything's amazing… as long as we can talk as much as possible, we cope fine with being apart. The girls always say he's so good to me.'

Zayn declared his love for Perrie during a Little Mix concert in Liverpool, screaming 'Love you, Perrie! Love you, Little Mix.' His mum Trisha has been to see lots of Little Mix concerts too and gets on really well with Perrie's mum, Debbie.

Perrie told the *Mirror*: 'Zayn is my best friend and I've seen more of him since we finished our tour but it's hard as One Direction have been on tour as well.

'But we went to The Brits together last month and had a great time.'

DID YOU KNOW?

When Zayn wanted a blond streak in his hair he got Perrie's mum to do it, as he explained on the Irish TV special, *The Story So Far*: 'I probably should have passed it with someone, but I didn't – I just cut it. I was sat at home and just decided I wanted a bit of a blond streak. My girlfriend's mum did it for me. She's a hairdresser, so it was cool.'

Both Perrie and Zayn do their best to ignore the negative stories in the press and to get on with living their lives; they try not to let the lies get to them and look forward to each time they can see each other. They enjoy having fun and are close friends, as well as boyfriend and girlfriend. Both come from loving, supportive families, who are behind them 110 per cent. Zayn enjoys spending time with Perrie's family although he was naturally a bit apprehensive the first time he met them. He told James Robertson from the *Mirror* in October 2012: 'I went up to meet her mum and family the other month. I was a bit scared of meeting her brother, to be honest – he's in the navy, he's a big bloke.

'I thought he was going to be a bit defensive over his sister but he was cool.'

In an interview Zayn's mum Trisha did with *Heat* magazine when she went to see Little Mix perform on *The X Factor*, she said: 'She would be a perfect daughter-in-law. I don't think we'll be seeing a proposal anytime soon, because they both want to focus on their careers.

'She's lovely, though. Zayn saw her on the telly and knew he liked her – he just had to convince her.

'Our families are each other's families now.'

When Harry, Liam, Louis, Niall and Zayn were interviewed by MTV they were asked who they thought would be first of the boys to walk down the aisle. Harry thought it would be Liam (Liam was dating Danielle Peazer at the time), but Liam thought that Zayn would be the most likely. He said: 'I reckon Zayn will do it spur of the moment.'

Niall agreed: 'Zayn would get married in Vegas.'

Louis wasn't sure who it would be, but said he would love it to be Niall as he is famous for saying things without thinking them through and could do it on the spur of the moment. He said: 'Imagine we just go away, have a year apart, doing whatever, all doing different things, and come back and Niall's just got married. I can see that happening.'

There was further speculation as to whether 'Zerrie' will be the first to tie the knot after Zayn got a tattoo of Perrie on his upper arm in June 2013. The tattoo was based on a sketch that Zayn had done and is a cartoon of Perrie wearing a bobble hat and CND T-shirt. He had it done while the boys were in Maryland, America. Perrie was shocked at first because she had had no idea that Zayn had been planning on getting a tattoo, but when she saw it she liked it.

At the *This Is Us* premiere on 20 August 2013 it was revealed that Zayn and Perrie were indeed engaged, as Perrie was wearing a diamond ring on her ring finger. A few days later Zayn admitted on the *Today Show*: 'There's not much to say… we are engaged, really happy.'

Perrie's mum Debbie told her local newspaper, the *Dorset Echo*: 'It's official. I'm over the moon. They are really in love… It's wonderful because Zayn is absolutely gorgeous. It's true they got engaged on Sunday and it's absolutely lovely. Perrie loves him to pieces and it's perfect. They get on so well together and understand each other. It's just fabulous.'

Zayn has lots of tattoos and is constantly adding to his collection. He got his Zap tattoo just because he loves comics, and for no other deep reason. He knows it's geeky but he was really into collecting comic books when he was younger. Some fans wrongly thought that he had his Zap tattoo because it stands for Zayn and Perrie. He has a pack of cards on his stomach with a crown and his initials on it, while 'be true to who you are' in Arabic appears on his left collarbone. Walter (his grandad's name) appears on his chest in Arabic, the yin and yang symbol on his wrist and a Japanese symbol on his hip, which means 'born lucky'. The crown tattoo on his chest stands for his surname 'Malik', which as we already know means 'King'. On his right forearm he has a 'fingers crossed' tattoo, which Zayn told *Seventeen* means, 'It's for the future – a hope that everything goes well.' He has a life-size microphone tattoo on his right forearm which he had done because singing and performing is so important to him, and always will be. On his lower stomach he used to have the Chinese symbol for 'born lucky' but had it changed to a heart. He has a silver fern on the back of his neck, which is a New Zealand symbol for good luck and a jigsaw piece near his elbow; he has quite a few number tattoos, too.

Zayn admits to being the bad boy of the group but thinks that he is misunderstood a lot of the time. In fact he is naturally quite awkward and shy. He loves his tattoos and is a bit addicted to getting new ones. He told *Now Magazine*: 'I want to fill my entire arm up to my elbow to start. I've got loads of ideas. I draw as well. I'm more addicted to coming up with the ideas of what I can get tattooed rather than the actual tattoo itself.'

He also revealed that Perrie is a fan, saying: 'Oh yeah! She likes my tats. She's into the whole rock 'n' roll look.'

DID YOU KNOW?

Zayn held Harry's hand when Harry had his first tattoo, a star, done by LA tattoo artist Freddy Negrete.

Trisha and the other 1D mums hope the boys don't get too many tattoos but at the moment they seem to be adding to their collections every few months. During an interview with *Daybreak*, Liam admitted: 'My mum went crazy about the whole tattoo idea.'

Zayn added: 'Simon [Cowell] hasn't said anything but our mums have been like, "Maybe you're getting a bit too much".'

Zayn is very close to his Mum – he loves her so much and always wants her to be happy. She's not at all controlling, and told the *Mirror* before Zayn got engaged to Perrie: 'Fans ask me for permission to marry him but he can choose his own Mrs.

'When he leaves home I cry at the gate and he says, "Mum! I'm not going to war!" A driver comes for him and I have to stand there and wave back at him. I go to London a lot and do all his washing.

'I don't expect Zayn to text me all the time, but I text him "Night, night, son" and he texts back, "Love you, Mum".'

CHAPTER EIGHT

FAN LOVE

Zayn likes to think there are three types of One Direction fan – those who scream, the ones who want to talk to them and those who don't say a word. He has seen a few fans faint the second they see him and the other boys, something he finds a bit daunting – he doesn't want to see anyone get hurt. He told *We Love Pop* about one particular incident: 'Obviously you don't get to see things like that unless you are The Beatles, who have that power, and to see it that close was a bit scary. I didn't really enjoy her fainting in front of me, however it was cool to know I could make a girl faint!'

Harry likes to suggest that Zayn has kissed the most fans but it must be a close call as all the boys hug and kiss fans on the cheek whenever they can. Zayn genuinely cares about all Directioners and appreciates every card, letter, drawing and present he is sent. If you want to write to Zayn, the address you need is:

ZAYN MALIK

Modest Management
The Matrix Complex
91 Peterborough Road
London SW6 3BU

Zayn doesn't want fans spending lots of money on presents but if you are talented at drawing, why not send him a sketch or two?

Zayn thinks that the lengths some fans will go to meet him, Harry, Niall, Liam and Louis are extreme. He has seen fans hide in garbage bins, pretend to work in the hotels where they are staying and chase down their van in busy traffic. But he doesn't like fans risking their safety and would prefer it if they attended official signings instead.

Zayn and the other boys have been interviewed thousands of times in countries across the globe, which means that often they have to answer the same questions again and again. That's why he likes it when interviewers ask the fans to submit questions they want to be answered because it means they will be asked something unique. During one Canadian interview the radio host refused to talk to Zayn because he claimed to have been given a list of questions and topics he couldn't discuss with Zayn by a member of One Direction's press team. The banned questions included: 'Who came up with the name

One Direction?', 'Which members of the group have girlfriends?' and 'Who is your celebrity crush?' These were all questions that fans already knew the answers to.

The radio host said goodbye and hung up on Zayn without asking a single question. Naturally this disappointed a lot of fans, who had been looking forward to hearing the interview. Zayn received a lot of criticism in the press over the interview but it wasn't his fault. He explained to Scott Mills on BBC Radio 1 in a later interview: 'The reason she [the press team member] was saying you can't ask these questions is because of the fans.

'They want to hear some new things; they want to know what's going on. They don't want to hear the same things over and over again. We always get asked the same questions so we just thought we'd mix it up a bit and try and rule out a few questions so we get some new ones.'

In May 2012 the boys released the *Up All Night* Tour DVD, allowing fans that couldn't get tickets for the tour the opportunity to see the show. Before it was released they organised a special performance for some of their biggest fans in America. They invited the fans to a special screening of the DVD at an American diner, only for Zayn and the other boys to turn up unannounced and perform for them.

The girls were simply chatting to each other in the booths or on stools by the counter when Zayn, Louis, Liam, Niall and Harry suddenly appeared and started singing 'What Makes You Beautiful' accompanied by an acoustic guitar. The girls couldn't believe their eyes and were so happy.

Afterwards Harry admitted to the cameras: 'I think when we play to like, intimate crowds, I think a lot of our songs are really fun and kind of high energy, so when we do it acoustic it's nice to kinda slow it down and have less people and just, you know, make it a little more personal and less about the atmosphere and more about the people in the room.'

Niall added: 'It's the people you get there – you get a natural reaction out of them because it's much more relaxed and you know, they feel a bit more privileged or whatever to be in a smaller room with just us. So it's quite nice.'

The boys were thrilled in November 2012 to announce that they were to release a 3D documentary movie titled *This Is Us* for their fans to see what it's like behind the schemes as they travel the world. Zayn explained to *Heat* magazine: 'It's just going to be the stuff you don't get to see – the day-to-day waking up in the morning, actually travelling.'

This Is Us was to be released worldwide on 30 August 2013 and fans couldn't wait. The movie was to be directed by Morgan Spurlock, who is most famous for his documentary movie *Super Size Me* (2004), which saw him eat three McDonald's meals a day for 30 days to see the effect it had on his body. Spurlock was really excited about the forthcoming movie, telling the press: 'This is an incredible opportunity and an amazing moment in time for the band. To capture this journey and share it with audiences around the world will be an epic undertaking that I am proud to be a part of.'

Simon Cowell added: 'I'm delighted we're making this film and Morgan is the perfect person to give that access-all-areas, behind-the-scenes look into what it's like to be One Direction today. What the band have achieved is incredible. They and their fans have made history around the world – this is for them.'

When the trailer for the movie was released in June 2013 fans heard a snippet of the boys' new track 'Best Song Ever', which is from their third album, *Midnight Memories*.

FAN LOVE

DID YOU KNOW?

Zayn would like Luke Pasqualino (Freddie from the TV series *Skins*) to play him, if a feature film was ever made about the band.

CHAPTER NINE

FAMILY
TIME

Family will always be the most important thing in Zayn's life and he will always put them before anything else. He admitted to *The Sun* how difficult it is to be travelling the world and to be apart from his mum, dad and sisters, saying: 'It's really been hard. Last weekend was the first time in six months that I've been home.

'I do feel like I've missed out a bit because I was really close with my sisters when I was at home. It must be weird for them but they cope really well.'

In 2013, his mum Trisha won an Inspirational Mum Award from her local council because of the way she has raised her children and the fact that she is an inspiration to other mums in Bradford. On the competition website there is an interview with Trisha. In it, she says: 'As a child I grew up in a very close-knit family. Born in a traditional white British working-class family, and as I grew up, I married a lovely British Pakistani man and became part of a loving British Muslim family. Coming from a completely different upbringing and background I have always tried to learn as much as I can about my husband's religion and culture, so that I can ensure my children maintain their British values and also learn about their father's roots and religious values. Integration and learning other languages and religion I must admit has been difficult, but I am happy to say I have a very happy family, both from my husband's side and from my family side.

'I have four children – three daughters aged 21, 14 and 10, and a son aged 20. My son has recently achieved huge success within the music industry, yet I try my best to ensure my children continue to remain humble and remember their early years of growing up in East Bowling. I brought up my family with very little money, living in a rented property in East Bowling. I have been working at Lowerfields Primary School for the last three years as a Halal Chef and continue to do so, despite my son's superstar success. I have always allowed my children the complete freedom to follow whatever they feel comfortable with, however I have also ensured that they have an understanding and knowledge of both mine and my husband's cultures and religions. As well as supporting my son with his music I have also made sure and encouraged his education at mosque and school. I continue to support my husband and family by working at a school and despite my family's new success, I remain local in Bradford. My son's success has changed things for me and my family, and it has become difficult for my family and I to try and maintain a normal life, however the future of my children is important and I feel as a mother my role is more difficult now to ensure I maintain the stability they have grown up with and that I am always there for them to ensure they cope with the change that has entered their lives.'

Zayn must have been so proud of his mum when she picked up her award, as she was such a deserving winner. He might be thousands of miles away from his family most of the time but he is always in mobile contact and knows he can contact them any time of day or night. In August 2012, he loved having the opportunity to take Perrie to Bradford to celebrate Eid with his family. Eid is a time when Muslims celebrate the end of Ramadan, which is the ninth month of the Islamic calendar, and when fasting is observed. A photo of them all together was shared on Twitter and although 1D fans sent them lovely comments, they also received lots of abuse from racist trolls.

Zayn was upset and admits that is partly why he deleted his Twitter account. He told the *Mirror*: 'I believe that your religion should be between you and whoever your belief is in.

'I don't think you should stick it in people's faces. I think you should just keep it to yourself and that's how I've always been with it. I just had seen a few things that had annoyed me.

'I thought we had moved away from that and we're living in the 21st century and people could accept people from different religions. It shouldn't have wound me up but it did.'

Zayn decided to go back on Twitter when he thought of all the millions of fans who would be disappointed. As he explained: 'There are so many fans on there who say nice things every day, so why should they miss out?'

DID YOU KNOW?

Some of Zayn's favourite 1D performances are when his family come to see him. He told *Daybreak*: 'It's really nice

> just to like, look out [at a concert] and see your family, however embarrassing they're being.
>
> 'Even if they're on the chair dancing, like, it's just cool.'

No matter where he is in the world, if there is a family emergency then Zayn will drop everything and fly home. In March 2012 his auntie died and he flew back home as soon as he could to support his family and to attend her funeral. This meant that he missed some concerts in North America so the boys had to adapt the show to cover his parts. The other boys understood completely why Zayn had to be with his family. Harry tweeted: 'Zayn has suffered a loss in his family & has had to go home for a few days so won't be at our next shows in the US.'

Zayn's family live normal lives and his mum, as stated previously, still goes to work every day and lives the life she lived before her son was famous. She does occasionally get recognised when she goes shopping and she finds it funny when girls ask if they can have a photo taken with her. Trisha told *ITV News*: 'The worst time for me is if I go to Zayn's tour. I do get stopped outside and they say, "Can we have a photo with you?" It's quite flattering when people stop you and say, "Can I have a photo with Zayn's mum or Zayn's sisters?" It's quite scary, really, sometimes. I think we were in Wolverhampton, and me and my daughter had to be removed from security, because all the fans just stood up, and it was quite scary to think that you're going to get mobbed by all the fans. So we had to be removed and moved up to a balcony.'

When Zayn tweets to say that he is going home to Bradford to see his family some fans turn up on Trisha's doorstep and leave him gifts or tie things to their gate, but they never leave too many items so it doesn't impact on the family very much. Trisha enjoys chatting to fans and finding out what songs they like, and talking about Zayn. Of course she is extremely proud of her famous son.

CHAPTER TEN

TOURING

The boys love touring and they get really excited every time a new tour is announced. Of course the first tour they took part in was the *X Factor* Live Tour, which ran from February to April 2011. They then embarked on their first solo UK and Ireland tour, which began in December 2011 and ended in January 2012. The 'Up All Night' Tour was later extended to include Australia, New Zealand, America, Canada and Mexico – this leg of the tour started in April 2012 and ended on 31 July 2012. In 2013 the boys embarked on their worldwide 'Take Me Home' Tour, which began in England in February 2013 and ended in Australia in October 2013. The tour included concerts in the UK, Ireland, France, Belgium, The Netherlands, Germany, Denmark, Norway, Sweden, Switzerland, Italy, Spain, Portugal, Mexico, America, Canada,

Australia and New Zealand. Their 2014 'Where We Are' Tour starts in Latin America in April 2014, before the boys return to UK and Ireland stadiums. When the tour was announced at Wembley Stadium on 16 May 2013, Harry told the press: 'It's important the fans and everyone who comes to see the show know it's going to be much bigger and new songs. A completely different tour.'

Zayn struggles being away from his family when the boys are touring but they do try and come to see him whenever they can. It helps having Harry, Niall, Liam and Louis going through the same thing – it would be much tougher if Zayn was a solo artist, because naturally he wouldn't have the same level of support. Being on tour and travelling the world means that the five of them have long days and spend a lot of time on the road. Zayn confessed to the *Daily Star*: 'I would have cracked up and gone home by now. There's defo no way I could have done this as a solo artist.

'The lads keep me grounded and it's good to know you're not the only person going through everything.'

DID YOU KNOW?

Zayn likes to wear two pairs of socks at once and during the 'Up All Night' Tour in America, he would ride a mini-scooter from their dressing room to the canteen.

For Zayn performing live is the best thing about touring but his second favourite thing is being on the 1D tour bus. He told Orlando radio station Mix105.1: 'My best experience of touring is being on the tour bus – like, just chilling out… like, after the show, when you get off the stage and you're on the tour bus, chilling out, that's cool.'

To combat boredom when travelling the boys love playing

pranks on each other. One day Harry shaved 'HS' into Zayn's leg hair when he was asleep and Zayn shaved a slit into Liam's eyebrow. To prank Niall, Zayn decided to put lemon juice on his new trainers, which turned them yellow. Niall was so mad! When they are walking around (or on stage) the bandmates sometimes pull each other's trousers down, which never fails to get a reaction. Arriving in Sweden, the other boys hid Zayn's luggage so he thought that he had left his things back in England.

When Harry turned 18 the boys were in LA so Zayn, Niall, Liam and Louis decided to play a prank on him. They were staying at the luxurious W Los Angeles – Westwood Hotel and booked Harry in for a massage. Harry was finding it all very relaxing until the boys came in halfway through and threw iced water at him!

The best prank Zayn has ever played was when he and Louis managed to convince Harry, Niall and Liam that an actress pretending to be a Nickelodeon producer was about to give birth. They were sitting together on couches in the TV studio and the woman asked them all to sing to the baby because that would stop it kicking on her bladder so much. The boys started to sing 'Rock-a-bye Baby' but then the actress began making noises and asked them to help because the baby was coming. Louis' mum was a nurse, so he went out to ring her for advice on what they should do, while the other boys tried to help the woman to her feet. Harry was the most shocked and tried to help the apparent mother-to-be in any way he could, telling Niall to go and get people to help. He had no idea that they were secretly being filmed with hidden cameras.

Poor Liam tried to speak to the lady's husband on her phone to let him know what was going on, but he got cut off. Meanwhile, Harry was trying to get her to breathe slowly. He couldn't help but snigger when Louis said it smelt, after which the woman admitted to having farted. Harry was very shocked when she said, 'You've all been pranked by Nickelodeon.' Zayn and Louis were so happy that they had managed to prank the others, they gave each other a hug and laughed at Harry's expense. If you haven't see the video clip for yourself, make sure you check it out on YouTube – it's hilarious!

When Zayn and the boys are touring they are looked after by Paul Higgins, who is their tour manager and has worked with the likes of Westlife, Boyzone and Girls Aloud. If you are on Twitter, you should follow Paul because he is always posting up interesting backstage photos and talking about what the boys are up to. His Twitter account is twitter.com/paulyhiggins. Paul is like a second dad to Zayn, Harry, Liam, Louis and Niall. He cares about them on a personal level, as well as professionally too. The boys went over to Ireland to see Paul marry his wife Clodagh in 2011 and filmed two really funny 'Marryoake' videos while they were there. Zayn and the rest of the boys appear on a karaoke-style video set to 'I've Gotta Feeling' by the Black Eyed Peas and Niall and Liam appear on a karaoke-style video set to 'Perfect Day' by Lou Reed.

Zayn and the boys have performed so many times in front of huge audiences but they still get a bit nervous before they walk on stage. They combat their nerves by trying to make each other laugh and by wishing one another good luck. Zayn admitted on YTV One to One what they get up to once they have done a soundcheck and have a break. He said: 'We just mess about, we're normal lads. We just mess about in our dressing rooms. We play this game called Real Fruit Ninja – basically, what you do is throw the fruit in the air and you cut it in half.' He warns fans not to try it at home and says to get permission from an adult before touching sharp objects. The boys started playing the game because their dressing rooms always seemed to be stocked up with a bowl of fruit, a knife and a chopping board.

In the same interview the other boys named Zayn as the member of 1D who is most likely to chill out at home rather than go out partying, and Niall said that on their days off, Zayn likes just staying in.

DID YOU KNOW?

Zayn used to make sure he always brushed his teeth before going on stage. However, he thought it was a little bit strange so he doesn't do it any more.

One of the boys' craziest performances was at New York's Radio City Hall, because the fans watching them were so loud. When they were leaving the venue, fans surrounded their tour van and their security team had to try and move the girls back before they could drive off. The Directioners were going crazy, banging on the windows and jumping on the back bumper of the van.

Zayn has had the opportunity to meet some amazing people through being in One Direction. During their time in America he met Michelle Obama and her daughters, Malia and Sasha. At the GQ Awards he was able to see Johnny Depp, Bono from U2, Charlize Theron and many more top stars. One of the first famous actresses he ever met was Emma Watson because 1D were invited to a Harry Potter premiere during their time on *The X Factor*.

Zayn did have the opportunity to spend time with Johnny Depp on a separate occasion, though when he was invited to the actor's studio he backed out because he was really nervous and didn't want to embarrass himself in front of one of his heroes. Harry, Liam, Louis and Niall went without him and had a blast, performing some songs for Depp's daughter, Lily-Rose. Zayn confessed to *The Sun*: 'Hopefully, there will be a next time. The boys said he was totally cool. I kind of regret it for sure and the lads said I was a scaredy cat.

'Some of our fans get so excited or nervous when they meet us and that's how I was at the thought of being with Johnny. But instead of lapping it up and enjoying it, I ran the other way.'

Zayn loved it when Olly Murs flew out to be their supporting act on the American leg of their 'Up All Night' Tour. Murs had been runner-up on *The X Factor* in 2009 and had had several hit singles in the UK, including 'Please Don't Let Me Go', 'Thinking Of Me' and 'Heart Skips A Beat'. He became a really good friend of 1D during the six weeks he spent on the road with them and Directioners really liked him too, learning the words to his songs so they could sing along when he performed. Zayn now considers Olly to be like an older brother.

Olly told *USA Today* at the time: 'The [One Direction] fans are insane! Running after the bus, jumping from trash cans, just so infatuated with the guys... One Direction fans wanted to know who I was. American fans are brilliant!'

In an interview with MTV, Olly said: 'One Direction's fans, they literally found out I was supporting them. They went online, found out who I was, what songs I've done, my videos and then I walked out [at the] first gig in Detroit [and] everyone's just crazy.

'I was like, "This is insane! They don't even know who I am. How could they be doing this?"'

DID YOU KNOW?

Zayn actually saw his first concert with the boys when they were in LA, as they all went together to see Britney Spears. The other boys had been attending concerts for many years: for Niall and Louis, their first one was seeing Busted, for Liam, it was seeing the *Pop Idol* finalists and for Harry, it was Nickelback.

When the boys went to Japan they had a great time and on arrival, did a bit of late-night karaoke. They sang songs by Backstreet Boys, Jay-Z, Kenny Rogers and 50 Cent. The next day at the press conference they were all feeling a bit rough because they had had a late night and needed to adjust to the time difference (the flight had been 11 hours long). Zayn was feeling terrible and after twenty minutes had to leave so he could get some rest.

Their schedule in Japan was crammed with performances and interviews but they did have a small amount of free time. Zayn bought himself a hi-tech robot and sampled some tofu and sashimi. All the boys enjoyed visiting a noodle bar but they struggled to understand what was on the menu because of course it was all in Japanese. They enjoyed wearing matching red kimonos during their visit, too.

DID YOU KNOW?

If Zayn could learn to speak any language he would pick Spanish. Harry would choose sign language and Liam would choose Japanese.

Zayn does enjoy travelling around the world but sometimes it can be a bit too much and he just wants a break. Occasionally he gets fed up of living out of a suitcase and staying in hotel rooms, even if they are totally luxurious. He finds long interview days tiring and wishes that he could explore some of the amazing places they visit. However, he tries to make the most of any days off he has in a new country, and the boys have visited some amazing theme parks and landmarks in lots of different places.

DID YOU KNOW?

If Zayn had to spend three years on a desert island with three people, he would pick his girlfriend Perrie, his friend Danny and Louis.

When fans attend a 1D concert they see the boys messing around and having a laugh, as well as performing great songs. They don't see lots of dance routines because dancing isn't what One Direction are about – they are more concerned with the music and putting on a good show. Brian Friedman, the choreographer who worked with the boys on *The X Factor*, told *Heat* magazine that Zayn still isn't a natural dancer, saying: 'He's got rhythm, he can't learn choreography. He gets really intimidated and scared and can't remember it.'

Brian was asked whether he thought One Direction should do more dance routines and he replied: 'Absolutely not! They didn't do too well with dancing when I was working with them.

'It's not that they can't handle it – some are better than others, no names to be mentioned – but it's not what they're about. They're not a dancey boyband kind of thing, they're just about youth and exuberance and making girls swoon.'

Above: Zayn was just starting to get used to his new-found fame when the boys made an appearance outside of HMV in December 2010.

Below: On *This Morning* Zayn and the others were forced to put their culinary skills to the test. Louis and Harry look like they're enjoying it, and Niall's seen something funny!

Above: Zayn is pictured here on his way to the *X Factor* set in 2010 (*left*) and outside the American Music Awards in 2013 (*right*). Except for his facial hair and his new smart clothes, he looks almost exactly the same!

Below: It's a long way from the *X Factor*: The boys were showing off their awards at the 2012 MTV Video Music Awards.

Above: Zayn loves to do live shows, like this one on French radio, so that he can talk directly to his fans.

Below: One Direction had the honour of performing at the London Olympics closing ceremony – a once in a lifetime opportunity for them.

Above Left: On tour in New Zealand, Zayn gives a sultry look to the large crowd.

Above Right: Singing from the heart here in a live performance for *Good Morning America*.

Below: The boys love their fans, and they always want to give something back, like with this huge cheque to help stop bullying. Niall looks unhappy about something though – maybe he wanted a bigger one!

DID YOU KNOW?

If Zayn could travel back in time he would like to go back to see dinosaurs for about five minutes. Harry would go back to when the pyramids were being built.

When interviewed for *The X Factor Australia* the boys were asked what they would do if that day was their last day on earth. Zayn said he would go and see his family, Harry said he would go for a hot-air balloon ride and Louis said they would all skydive into their families' houses.

CHAPTER ELEVEN

FOOD
GLORIOUS
FOOD

Zayn loves eating and he is always up for trying something new or taking part in a food–related challenge. When he was living in the *X Factor* house he took some cookery lessons and played up to the cameras, pretending to be a cookery expert while wearing a black wig, but he didn't take the lessons very seriously and instead messed around with Louis. He also took part in a 'chilli challenge' with his fellow *X Factor* contestants Paije Richardson and John Adeleye. They had to eat four chillies and if they took a gulp of milk, they would be disqualified. John struggled with the second chilli, while Paije struggled with the third but all three managed to eat their four chillies without reaching for the milk! Zayn was by far the best though, because he ate them as if they weren't hot at all.

In another challenge (called 'Brain Freeze'), Zayn managed to beat Paije and Geneva from Belle Amie. The challenge involved seeing how many ice-cream shots they could take before experiencing 'brain freeze'. Geneva only managed two but Paije and Zayn ended up drawing, with four shots. To decide on a winner both had to eat three ice-cream shots without using their hands and the fastest person won. Zayn was the fastest, so he was declared the Brain Freeze champion!

While touring, the boys' food is prepared by chef Sarah Nicholas, who is in charge of making sure that they eat a varied, healthy diet. She lets them have their favourite meals but she cooks healthier versions. Sarah loves how Zayn isn't a fussy eater and likes dishes such as pasta bolognese and spicy chicken (chicken is Zayn's favourite food). She told the *Daily Star* that Louis' favourite food is Special K and that Niall likes 'sausage and mash, pies, creamy chicken pasta or chicken kiev.' She added that Louis drinks the most tea and the boys 'also drink more juices and water than fizzy drinks. Before they go onstage, they tend to have orange or apple juice, Capri-Suns or Rubicon.'

If you want to see some examples of the type of things she cooks for the boys, head to Sarah's website and check out her sample menus. Her website address is: www.sarahskitchentouring.com. She has cooked for comedian Peter Kay, Olly Murs, Il Divo, Elvis Costello, JLS, Will Young and many more stars.

DID YOU KNOW?

If Zayn could have dinner with anyone, dead or alive, it would be Michael Jackson. He would also like to invite David Beckham, Louis and Liam.

Of course the boys do eat out and have takeaways, as well as the food that Sarah prepares. When performing at Newcastle's

Metro Radio Arena, they ordered in the following dishes from Nandos:

> Zayn – 1 x double chicken pitta (medium) with cheese, 1 x mixed olives, 1 x coleslaw, 1 x corn on the cob, 1 x hot sauce, 1 x extra-hot sauce
>
> Harry – 1 x double chicken (mango & lime) wrap with cheese and pineapple
>
> Liam – Butterfly chicken (medium, no skin), mixed olives, 1 x Perinaise sauce
>
> Louis – 1 x half chicken (medium), 1 x creamy mash, 1 x Perinaise sauce
>
> Niall – 1 x double chicken wrap (medium, no lettuce), 1 x spicy rice, 5 x wings (medium), 1 x Perinaise, 1 x medium sauce

Sarah might be a great chef, but Zayn can't help but miss his mum Trisha's cooking when the boys are on tour. He told the *Sun* magazine: 'I love samosas filled with mincemeat – my mum makes really great ones.'

Niall loves her cooking too, adding: 'Zayn's mum makes such good food – I can eat so much!'

Zayn is a little bit jealous of how Niall can eat anything, telling *Top of the Pops* magazine: 'Niall is the skinniest… he just eats and eats and eats and eats. But he never puts any weight on!

'It's a little bit annoying. The rest of us have to watch what we eat, but Niall can eat just anything and be fine.'

CHAPTER TWELVE

TAKE ME HOME

Zayn loved promoting *Up All Night*, but he loved going into the studio to record the boys' second album even more. There might have been pressure for them to record an even better album than their first, but the boys were more than up to it. They were looking forward to working with Ed Sheeran and all the other amazing songwriters and producers they had worked with first time around. Now, however, they wanted *Take Me Home* to have more guitars than *Up All Night* because they had really enjoyed having guitars on their tour and they wanted to write more.

Zayn loves working with Ed and told Capital Radio: 'It's all just chilled – the whole vibe of his studio is chilled out.

'He's got a field and sometimes you just sit out on the field and jam with a guitar, play a little bit of football, walk into the studio when you feel like it, walk back out when you feel like it. It's wicked!'

DID YOU KNOW?

Zayn would love the opportunity to record a track with Justin Timberlake in the future. He is a huge Justin Timberlake fan and really rates his song SexyBack. He would also like to work with Chris Brown and Katy Perry one day.

In the build-up to the album being released the boys' press team gave the following statement to the media: 'The eagerly awaited second album is due for release in November 2012 and sees One Direction collaborating with a whole host of first-class writers and producers. As well as reuniting with the likes of Rami Yacoub & Carl Falk and Savan Kotecha, Ed Sheeran and McFly's Tom Fletcher, the album features input from Dr Luke, Shellback and Toby Gad. The album is sure to be another huge smash release from a truly international pop phenomenon.'

The first single Zayn and the boys released from the album was 'Live While We're Young'. It was available on pre-order from Friday, 24 August 2012. The track was by the three songwriters who penned 'What Makes You Beautiful' – Savan Kotecha, Rami Yacoub and Carl Falk.

'Live While We're Young' instantly became the fastest-selling pre-order single ever, topping iTunes download charts in 40 countries worldwide from the UK to Singapore, New Zealand to Mexico. The music video was directed by Vaughan Arnell, who was the director behind Robbie Williams's 'Rock DJ' video and the Spice Girls' 'Say You'll Be There' video. It was filmed in the Kent countryside over two days. In the video the boys are camping with their friends and have lots of fun playing football, riding in a jeep, having water fights, playing with inflatable balls and going for a dip in a paddling pool. Although great fun it wasn't at all glamorous – it got pretty cold while they messed about in the water.

Originally, the boys had been planning for the video to be released on 24 September but ended up releasing it four days earlier after someone posted a rough version online. In a statement, they said: 'We wanted our fans to see the video and hear the single in the proper way so we've moved the premiere to tonight. We're really excited about LWWY, we've worked really hard on it and we can't wait for everyone to see and hear it later today!'

DID YOU KNOW?

The video for 'Live While We're Young' was watched 8.24 million times in the first 24 hours of its release – a VEVO record!

TAKE ME HOME – TRACK BY TRACK

Track 1 – 'Live While We're Young' – was written by Rami Yacoub, Carl Falk and Savan Kotecha. It was produced by Rami Yacoub and Carl Falk.

Track 2 – 'Kiss You' – was written by Rami Yacoub, Carl Falk, Savan Kotecha, Shellback, Kristian Lundin, Albin Nedler and Kristoffer Fogelmark. It was produced by Rami Yacoub and Carl Falk.

Track 3 – 'Little Things' – was written by Ed Sheeran and Fiona Bevan. It was produced by Jake Gosling.

Track 4 – 'C'mon, C'mon' – was written by Jamie Scott, John Ryan and Julian C. Bunetta. It was produced by John Ryan and Julian C. Bunetta.

Track 5 – 'Last First Kiss' – was written by Albin Nedler, Kristoffer Fogelmark, Rami Yacoub, Carl Falk, Savan Kotecha, Liam, Zayn and Louis. It was produced by Rami Yacoub, Carl Falk, Albin Nedler and Kristoffer Fogelmark.

Track 6 – 'Heart Attack' – was written by Rami Yacoub, Carl Falk, Savan Kotecha, Shellback and Kristian Lundin. It was produced by Rami Yacoub, Carl Falk and Shellback.

Track 7 –'Rock Me' – was written by Lukasz Gottwald, Henry Walter, Peter Svensson, Allan Grigg and Sam Hollander. It was produced by Dr Luke, KoOoLkOjAk and Cirkut for Prescription.

Track 8 – 'Change My Mind' – was written by Rami Yacoub, Carl Falk and Savan Kotecha. It was produced by Rami Yacoub and Carl Falk.

Track 9 – 'I Would' – was written by Tom Fletcher, Danny Jones and Dougie Poynter. It was produced by Julian Bunetta, Sam Waters and John Ryan.

Track 10 – 'Over Again' – was written by Ed Sheeran, Robert Conlon and Alexander Gowers. It was produced by Jake Gosling.

Track 11 – 'Back for You' – was written by Kristoffer Fogelmark, Savan Kotecha, Albin Nedler, Rami Yacoub, Carl Falk, Liam, Harry, Louis and Niall. It was produced by Rami Yacoub, Carl Falk, Albin Nedler and Kristoffer Fogelmark.

Track 12 – 'They Don't Know About Us' – was written by Tebey Ottoh, Tommy Lee James, Peter Wallevik and Tommy P Gregersen. It was produced by Tebey Ottoh, Julian Bunetta and John Ryan.

Track 13 – 'Summer Love' – was written by Steve

Robson, Wayne Hector, Lindy Robbins and 1D. It was produced by Steve Robson.

Bonus tracks:

Track 14 – 'She's Not Afraid' – was written by Jamie Scott, John Ryan and Julian Bunetta. It was produced by John Ryan and Julian Bunetta.

Track 15 – 'Loved You First' – was written by Ottoh, Bunetta, Ryan, James. It was produced by John Ryan and Julian Bunetta.

Track 16 – 'Nobody Compares' – was written by Rami Yacoub, Carl Falk, Savan Kotecha and Shellback. It was produced by Rami Yacoub, Carl Falk and Shellback.

Track 17 – 'Still the One' – was written by Rami Yacoub, Carl Falk, Savan Kotecha, Liam, Louis and Harry. It was produced by Rami Yacoub, Carl Falk and Shellback.

WHAT THE REVIEWERS THOUGHT:

James Robertson from the *Mirror* wrote in his review: '…with tracks written by the genius Ed Sheeran and McFly's Tom Fletcher, this was never going to be a predictable pop album. There are some obvious rhymes and repetitive tones but the five-piece have smashed it with *Take Me Home*.

'It's fun, infectious and they've found the balance between poptastic fun for the pre-teens and lyrics with meaning for embarrassed twenty-somethings who secretly listen to *Up All Night* on their iPods.'

The HitFix.com reviewer loved the album, writing: 'The tunes, tailor-made for the 2013 arena tour the quintet has already sold out, are slightly more sophisticated than the tracks on *Up All Night*, but to the band's credit, they in no way attempt to leave behind the audience that made them so popular.

'There's a song factory working overtime that churns this stuff out and the overlords have names like Dr. Luke, Shellback and Ed Sheeran: in other words, 1D has the top pop crafters in the land coming up with these tunes.'

Billboard's reviewer wrote: 'Following the massive success of *Up All Night* and the single "What Makes You Beautiful," the *X Factor* judge and band advisor challenged pop's most dominant songwriters and producers to bring their A-game to One Direction's follow-up. A glance at the album's liner notes shows some familiar faces and some new ones, but most importantly, at least half of *Take Me Home*'s songs sound like potential singles, ranging from glossy electro-pop to sentimental acoustic ballads. Even with so many producers lending a hand, there isn't a dud to be found on the record's thirteen tracks. At worst, some of the lesser cuts sound like photocopies of their stronger counterparts, which is certainly a forgivable offence for the boys of One Direction.'

DID YOU KNOW?

Zayn let Perrie and her Little Mix bandmates, Jade, Jesy and Leigh-Anne, hear a sneak preview of the album before it was released. Jade confessed to Capital FM: 'I heard one. We heard a cheeky little song, but we're not allowed to say anything. It's brilliant – the fans will love it!'

Leigh-Anne added that she would like One Direction and Little Mix to do a track together one day. She said: 'I think it would be really interesting – a Little Mix and One Direction [song]. Imagine what that would be like.'

The boys went to Farley Hill in Henley-on-Thames to take promotional shots for the album and this is where they did the phone-box album cover shot. Zayn admitted to a VEVO backstage camera: 'Today is Wednesday, 11 July (2012), we're doing a photo shoot today for our next album. 6am start, got up, drove here; we've just been getting changed, getting into our looks… Found a golf buggy, decided to take to take that out for a bit.'

Take Me Home was released on 9 November 2012 in Australia, Germany and The Netherlands; the other release dates were: 12 November in the UK, 13 November in America and 14 November in Japan. It was No. 1 in America, Australia, Belgium, Canada, Croatia, Czech Republic, Denmark, Greece, Ireland, Italy, Mexico, The Netherlands, New Zealand, Norway, Portugal, Sweden, Switzerland, Taiwan, the UK and many more countries (32 in total). In Austria, Brazil, Finland, Germany and Hungary it was No. 2 and was No. 3 in France, Japan, Poland and Spain.

The album set two records in America as 1D were the first British group to have both their first and second album debut at No. 1 in the charts and it was an American iTunes pre-order record as fans pre-ordered an incredible 130,000 albums. *Take Me Home* was also No. 1 in the UK album chart and 'Little Things' was No. 1 in the UK singles chart at the same time. It was an amazing achievement and as soon as Zayn's mum found out, she texted him a message, saying: 'Congratulations, superstar' and he replied 'Thanks, mom and pop.'

She also texted: 'We're so happy, and that's not a little thing – no pun intended.'

The whole family had been listening to *The Official Chart Show* on Radio 1 and when they found out, they danced around the kitchen in excitement. They are all so proud of Zayn and keep newspaper and magazine cuttings for him so he can see good news articles about himself and the boys when he's home.

> **DID YOU KNOW?**
>
> Zayn's mum has a picture of him on her phone cover – she gets funny looks when people see it and don't realise who she is. They think she's old to have a crush on him!

The second single from *Take Me Home* that the boys released was 'Little Things', written by Fiona Bevan and Ed Sheeran. The video was directed by Vaughan Arnell, who shot the boys simply in black-and-white, singing the song in a Surrey recording studio. In the video, Niall, Liam and Louis play guitar. Vaughan explained to MTV: 'When I first heard the track, the mix on it was so simple and so pure and you could hear all the qualities of the voices on the track. I just wanted to come up with something that when the viewer watched it, it was almost like sitting there listening to the boys sing the track.'

They shot the video on 15 October 2012 and it took 12 hours in total, with the boys having to sing over and over so Vaughan could get shots from every angle. It must have been very tiring and difficult to stay focused for that length of time. Zayn didn't mind, though and tweeted the next day: 'Shooting video for little things was fun yesterday! Nice and sunny today, how is every1 doing? :) x'

Fans got to see the video for the first time on 2 November and '#LittleThingsOnVEVO' was soon the No. 1 trending topic on Twitter worldwide. It was released on 12 November 2012 and was No. 1 in the UK, No. 2 in Ireland and New Zealand, No. 5 in Israel, No. 9 in Australia and charted well in other countries too.

The third single they released was 'Kiss You', the second single from the album to be released in Germany and America. 'Kiss You' was written by a team of songwriters that included

Savan Kotecha, Carl Falk and Rami Yacoub. The music video couldn't have been any more different to the 'Little Things' video. High-energy and fun, it showed the boys goofing around and was once again directed by Vaughan Arnell. This time he had them recreate scenes from famous music videos using a green screen. They did their own take of Elvis Presley's 'Jailhouse Rock' and the Beach Boys' 'Surfer Girl'.

DID YOU KNOW?

The video was shot at the studio where *Star Wars* was filmed, in Borehamwood.

Liam told MTV why they decided that the track should be their second release in America. He explained: 'With the album, that's the first one that we listened to and we were like, "Yeah, we love this song".

'It holds a special place in our heart, I think, for this album, and it kind of sets the tone, I think, for the album.'

Zayn added: 'I think the whole concept behind the video is bigger than anything we've done before. It's a whole idea and it's kind of structured, which is a little bit different than what we've done before in, like, a comedy way. It's really funny – we are just having fun.'

The song charted at No. 7 in Ireland, No. 9 in the UK, No. 13 in Australia, Mexico and New Zealand, and No. 46 in America.

CHAPTER THIRTEEN

SPECIAL
MOMENTS

For Zayn, there have been so many special moments in the last few years that it's hard for him to choose some favourites. He told Billboard.com: 'It is so hard to put into words what 2012 has meant to us. Last year was an amazing year for us, but when our debut album went to No. 1 over here [America] we were blown away by that. We didn't expect any of the support to the kind of level we were getting out there in the UK. And then we come out eight months later with our second album over here and it goes to No. 1 again. Things like that don't happen and we know that. We're incredibly humbled by that. Wow, what can we say except for thank you to the fans who went out and bought it.'

One moment that Zayn will never forget is when 1D performed at the 2012 *Royal Variety Performance* and he shook the Queen's hand afterwards. They performed 'Little Things' on specially created light boxes, with Zayn in the middle. To start the song, knowing that millions of people were watching the historic show, was a big moment for Zayn. Only the very best acts get invited to perform at a Royal Variety show and it was the 100-year anniversary so it was such a special night. Other performers who shared the stage included the legendary Rod Stewart, Neil Diamond, Robbie Williams, Girls Aloud, Kylie Minogue, Alicia Keys and Andrea Bocelli. Having to line up afterwards and wait for HM the Queen to go along the line, chatting to the performers, was nerve-wracking, but Zayn did so well. It's not every day you get to meet the Queen of England and shake her hand!

Zayn was very excited when he found out that he and the other boys were getting their own waxwork models in Madame Tussauds. It was a complete surprise when he found out – the boys were visiting Madame Tussauds at the time. He never expected it because you have to be a legend to be included, since each individual model costs £150,000 to make, as they must be exact replicas. Even though 1D are worldwide stars, Zayn always thinks of them as being normal lads.

DID YOU KNOW?

During their trip to Madame Tussauds the boys picked their favourite waxworks. For Zayn, it had to be Bob Marley, but for Louis it was the model of The Beatles. Harry liked Gandhi, Niall loved the Rihanna model the best, while the Arnold Schwarzenegger waxwork got Liam's vote.

Before the 1D models were unveiled, principal sculptor Stephen Mansfield revealed in a video for the Madame Tussauds website: 'We are acutely aware that millions of fans around the world will have a lot to say about these figures and we are determined not to let them down. We are hard at work to not only recreate totally accurate physical likenesses, but we want to inject something of the boys' energy and personalities into their figures too. The boys have been a delight to work with, really co-operative and a huge amount of fun.'

The waxworks were available for viewing in the London Madame Tussauds from 28 April to 11 July 2013, before being transported to the New York Madame Tussauds for American fans to check them out from 19 July to 11 October and then they went all the way to the Madame Tussauds in Sydney, Australia from 24 October 2013 to 28 January 2014.

To see exclusive content about the models and read interviews with the boys, check out www.madametussauds.com/1D

DID YOU KNOW?

The waxwork Zayn, Niall, Liam, Louis and Harry all have their arms covered with long sleeves, which will stop the models from becoming dated, since the boys are constantly adding tattoos to their arms. It would be very time-consuming for the sculptors to add their new tattoos all the time!

One of Zayn's favourite moments from 2013 was attending the BRIT Awards on 20 February and winning the BRITS Global Success Award, which was presented to the boys by Robbie Williams. Previously, they had won the Best Single Award in 2012 for 'What Makes You Beautiful'. Before the 2013 ceremony Zayn went for a haircut, while Harry went for a massage. On the red carpet Zayn was asked by Capital FM if he was nervous. He replied: 'Yeah, massively...

We're up against some massive names, we're just honoured to be here.'

On the night they also performed their mash up of the Blondie song 'One Way Or Another' and The Undertones' 'Teenage Kicks' – their Comic Relief charity single. Zayn was thrilled when the song went to No. 1 because it raised £2 million for charity. The boys actually visited Ghana to see how the money would be spent and Zayn broke down in tears when he saw the suffering and poverty children in the slums have to deal with. Liam summed up how they all felt by saying: 'It must be so difficult seeing your baby so ill. At home we take vaccinations for granted but not all children here have access to them and that can mean the difference between life and death. I've watched Red Nose Day appeals before and been in tears but seeing these babies so sick is another level of sadness.'

For Zayn his visit to Ghana is something he will never, ever forget and he will continue to raise money for good causes. He told *Daybreak*: 'It kind of put things into perspective for me, just in, like in everyday life you have, like, little problems that we think are so major, and then you go over there and you actually see people that are actually dealing with real problems.'

The boys have won so many awards that it is impossible to list them all, but each one is special to them, especially those voted for by the fans. They loved winning two People's Choice awards in LA in January 2013 for Favourite Song ('What Makes You Beautiful') and Favourite Album (*Up All Night*). Attending the 2012 Bambi Awards in Dusseldorf, Germany in November 2012 was fun – they performed 'Live While We're Young' and won the Pop International Award. They were thrilled to win three awards (Best New Act, Best UK and Ireland Act and Best Fans) at the November 2012 MTV EMAs (European Music Awards) in Frankfurt and although they couldn't be there in person, they recorded a thank you message for the fans.

One of their biggest victories was at the MTV Video Music Awards in LA on 6 September 2012. The boys picked up three awards: Best New Artist, Best Pop Video and Most Share-Worthy Video (all for 'What Makes You Beautiful'). They performed 'One Thing' and say that attending the VMAs made them think they had arrived. They never expected to win the awards and right up until the last minute had been asking fans to vote. The person they liked meeting the most was Lil Wayne, although Niall would say Katy Perry because they kissed on the lips! Simon Cowell was very proud, tweeting them to say, 'Congratulations 1D. I'm very proud of you. Celebrate!'

Celebrate they certainly did, as after they'd won their first award Zayn and Niall had a chat in their dressing room. Zayn told Niall: 'There's no way we can win a MTV Video Music Award and go home.' Niall agreed and the two of them attended Justin Bieber's aftershow party and stayed in America for a few more days before catching a flight back to the UK. Zayn hurt his foot during their extended stay so when the paparazzi took lots of photos at the airport, he decided to reassure Directioners that he was okay. He tweeted: 'Hey guys, just to let you all know I'm all good, no need to worry aha.

'Just wanna take a moment to thank you guys for being so amazing.

'I've said it so many times but ill say it again, you really are the best fans in the world, thank you for being so incredible. Love you all :x'

CHAPTER FOURTEEN

ZAYN'S BEST TWEETS:

'Vas sapnin had a great malik monday! Bedtime for me now, x'
'Live for who and what you love … and never compromise your beliefs for anything or anyone .. x'
'I love the fact I grew up wanting a brother and now I have four love u boys man :)'
'Learn from yesterday, live for today and hope for tomorrow, x'
'Children in need was amazing tonight lets try raise as much we can :D x'
'Just before I go to bed just want to say Happy Birthday to one of musics biggest inspirations, Michael Jackson, you truly were a legend RIPx'
'London!!! Smashed it amazing show thankyou directioners never fail to impress me with there lung capacity u guys can scream ! #amazingfans!'
'Night guys, X x X and remember live learn and love xx'

Why don't you flip over the book and read *Liam Payne: The Biography*?

LIAM
PAYNE

LIAM PAYNE

THE BIOGRAPHY

SARAH OLIVER

JOHN BLAKE

Published by John Blake Publishing Ltd,
3 Bramber Court, 2 Bramber Road,
London W14 9PB, England

www.johnblakepublishing.co.uk

www.facebook.com/Johnblakepub facebook
twitter.com/johnblakepub twitter

This edition published in 2014

ISBN: 978 1 78219 751 5

British Library Cataloguing-in-Publication Data:

A catalogue record for this book is available from the British Library.

Design by www.envydesign.co.uk

Printed and bound in Great Britain by CPI Group (UK) Ltd

1 3 5 7 9 10 8 6 4 2

Papers used by John Blake Publishing are natural, recyclable products made from
wood grown in sustainable forests. The manufacturing processes conform to the
environmental regulations of the country of origin.

Every attempt has been made to contact the relevant copyright-holders, but some
were unobtainable. We would be grateful if the appropriate people could contact us.

ABOUT THE AUTHOR

Sarah Oliver is a writer from Widnes in Cheshire. She was the author of the first ever book on Zayn, Niall, Liam, Louis and Harry, entitled *One Direction A–Z*, which was a *Sunday Times* bestseller. She also wrote the double biography of Harry Styles and Niall Horan, the book *One Direction Around the World*, and appeared in the documentary, *One Direction – All For One*.

Why not follow Sarah – @SarahOliverAtoZ – on Twitter?

Dedicated with love to Bethany and Ellie

CONTENTS

If you love One Direction then you should follow the boys on Twitter. Here are the Twitter addresses you need:

One Direction – http://twitter.com/onedirection
Liam – https://twitter.com/Real_Liam_Payne
Zayn – https://twitter.com/zaynmalik
Harry – http://twitter.com/harry_styles
Niall – https://twitter.com/NiallOfficial
Louis – https://twitter.com/Louis_Tomlinson

Other interesting people connected to Liam,
who you might want to follow:
His best friend Andy – https://twitter.com/AndySamuels31
Liam's friend Tom – https://twitter.com/tomqueens
Liam's sister Ruth – https://twitter.com/RuthPayne0990
One Direction's hairstylist Lou Teasdale –
http://twitter.com/louteasdale

1993: A STAR IS BORN!

Liam was born at New Cross Hospital in Wolverhampton on 29 August 1993. He is the third oldest member of One Direction, with Louis and Zayn being older than him and Niall and Harry younger. He was a much welcome addition to the Payne family. His mum Karen had him at thirty-seven weeks, which is three weeks early. Liam's birth was traumatic for nursery nurse Karen and his dad Geoff (who is a Goodrich aerospace fitter) because Liam was unconscious when he was born and he almost died. He wasn't very well at all and it took four years for doctors to figure out what was wrong with him. It turned out he only had one functioning kidney and the kidney that worked wasn't functioning at 100 per cent capacity.

Karen and Geoff gave Liam the middle name James, which incidentally is the same middle name as Niall's parents gave him. Liam was Karen and Geoff's first son (they already had two girls, Ruth and Nicola). They showered him with love and the girls loved playing with Liam and winding him up. They gave him the nickname 'Cheesy Head' because he loved eating cheese crisps. The girls would also use Liam as their own doll and dress him up in heels and dresses. Liam didn't mind too much at the time because he was so young but now he finds the memory a bit embarrassing. He and his sisters also used to write letters to the tooth fairy but one day Liam caught his mum writing a reply and he couldn't understand what was going on.

Growing up, Liam really wanted to be a fireman because he thought they had a cool job. One day he went past a fire station and the firemen had moved their engines out of the building so they were lined up outside and the firemen themselves were inside, playing tennis on a court they had set up. He thought being a fireman would be so much fun!

Liam was a happy child but because of his kidney trouble he was in pain a lot of the time. It was really hard on Karen and Geoff to see their son in pain because of his health issues and they had to give him up to 64 injections a day to try and help ease the pain. Poor Liam had to be so brave to get through it.

DID YOU KNOW?

When Liam got older he decided not to drink alcohol and to follow a healthy lifestyle to protect his functioning kidney (and also because he doesn't like the taste of beer). In August 2013 he discovered that his kidney had miraculously fixed itself, tweeting: 'Just been for an ultrasound on my kidney turns out its fixed from when I was a baby!!! :o so now I have two :) #weirdnewsoftheday.'

Liam went to Collingwood Primary School in Wolverhampton. He was really cheeky and loved pushing the boundaries. He had water fights in the toilets with his friends and they enjoyed messing around. Liam loved sport so he tried to join the different teams but never managed to get in until he gave running a shot. Normally it takes a lot of training to become a good long-distance runner but it all came naturally to Liam and he came first in his debut long-distance race. He even managed to beat a boy who ran for the city team!

With support from his parents Liam decided to pursue running and started training as hard as he could without allowing it to affect his schoolwork. Unlike other young boys who need encouragement to get out of bed so they can get to school on time, Liam used to jump out of bed, get changed and head out on a run. He would run for miles and miles before returning home and swapping his shorts and T-shirt for his school uniform. He even ran in the school holidays and when he was visiting his grandad Ken in Cornwall.

Liam continued running when he left Collingwood Primary School and moved to St Peter's Collegiate School, just a few days after his eleventh birthday. While focused on his running, he also gave other sports a try. He joined the basketball team and enjoyed going to see West Bromwich Albion play at weekends at The Hawthorns stadium. Because he loved playing basketball and singing, he thought he was a bit like Troy from the *High School Musical* movies. His parents thought he would one day make a good PE teacher.

While at high school Liam took up boxing for self-defence after he was bullied. Sometimes he needed to escape the bullies and would miss school. He might have only been 12 but he enjoyed getting in the ring with his 24-year-old coach, even if he got a bit battered and bruised. Liam had to fit his boxing

3

in around his running as he was by now training with the Wolverhampton and Bilston Athletics team as well. His running times got faster and faster, making him one of the fastest boys of his age in the whole of the UK.

DID YOU KNOW?

Liam sometimes has very strange dreams. He told the *Sun*: 'I dream of being back at school a lot and have been naked a few times. And I have been in the park naked on a climbing frame.'

When Liam was fourteen he was devastated when he found out that he hadn't got a place in the England Schools team so he decided to leave running and pursue his singing ambitions instead. He told journalist Victoria Nash: 'I used to get up and run five miles before school and another few miles when I came home. At that time it was always a choice between running or singing, but I just missed out on a place in the England team. I didn't enjoy the running as much as my singing and that really made my mind up for me.'

DID YOU KNOW?

Liam is the most competitive member of One Direction, partly because of his running experiences. He loved to win at running and he loves it when 1D do well too.

Liam really suffered at the hands of the bullies at school who were jealous of him. He nearly got expelled after having the courage to stand up to them one day. Thankfully this didn't happen and he was permitted to stay in school. His bullies must be even more jealous of Liam now that he is a worldwide star!

Liam started out singing karaoke when he was on holiday

with his family abroad. He told the backstage *X Factor* cameras: 'I first started singing when I was about six years old, maybe earlier than that, singing R. Kelly "I Believe I Can Fly" on karaoke, which I put myself in for. You couldn't even see me behind the DJ desk, that's how small I was.' He also liked singing to Robbie Williams and Oasis songs; his sister Ruth enjoyed singing with him too. Liam also sang in the school choir. He explained: 'I've always loved singing – it's something I've always done, ever since I first got up on karaoke when I was at holiday camp and mumbled the words to Robbie Williams's "Let Me Entertain You".' Although he was only six years old, he had lots of confidence. His mum made sure the performance was videoed so she could replay it when she got home.

DID YOU KNOW?

Liam set a world record with his school friends when they took part in a performance alongside other school choirs. They all had to sing 'Lean On Me' by Bill Withers at the same time. Michael Coates used to sing in the school choir with Liam and when they were in their early teens they entered a school talent competition together. They sang R. Kelly's 'If I Could Turn Back The Hands Of Time'. Until Year 8 or 9 not many people knew that Liam was a great singer, they just thought he was a runner.

Michael and Liam are still really close and Michael was gutted for his friend when he didn't make *The X Factor Live* shows in 2008. The two of them went to meet JLS with another friend called Sam when Marvin, Aston, JB and Oritsé were in Wolverhampton doing a gig. Michael told the *Express & Star*: 'We went to their hotel, the Britannia. Liam told them we used to sing together and he got me to sing the R. Kelly song. I couldn't believe I was singing to JLS!'

When Liam was twelve he decided to join a performing arts group called Pink Productions with his sister. His dance teacher Jodie Richards told the *Birmingham Mail*: 'Who'd have thought the Liam we see today would have nearly had to be forced onto the stage? It was clear very early that Liam was a natural talent. He gained more and more confidence with each show and took on some big singing numbers. Liam is such a lovely lad and I'm very proud to say I know him and have so many fantastic memories of him from rehearsals and personal experiences.'

Liam admits if it wasn't for Jodie and everyone at Pink Productions then he wouldn't have had the confidence for *The X Factor* first time around. He was fourteen when he first auditioned in 2008, as the *X Factor* producers had decided to lower the age range (in future series, the minimum age was raised back to sixteen). Liam told the *X Factor* cameras at the time: 'When I'm at school, in general I think about singing all the time. I should really be concentrating on my work but I just think about singing too much. It's a dream and I'd love to do it!'

DID YOU KNOW?
Liam's first ever pet was a terrapin called Frederick.

For the 2008 series of *The X Factor* in the first round the acts had to face judges Simon Cowell, Cheryl Cole and Louis Walsh. They didn't have to sing in front of an audience at all but this was still a daunting thing to do because Liam had only a couple of minutes to impress them. He had to secure two yeses to make it through to Bootcamp. As soon as he introduced himself, Liam was asked by Louis: 'Why are you here?'

Liam replied: 'I'm here to win. A lot of people have said I'm a good singer and I've got the X Factor but I don't really know what the X Factor is and I believe that you guys do.'

DID YOU KNOW?

Liam's audition number was 59461. In total, 182,000 people applied for that year's *X Factor*.

The song Liam chose to sing was the classic 'Fly Me To The Moon' by Frank Sinatra. He had picked a mature track and looked grown up, too – he was wearing an open-collared shirt with a waistcoat and smart jeans. It was a good choice of song as Louis commented, 'Simon loves Swing.' Liam was very confident in his performance, clicking his fingers and even winking at Cheryl at one point. She looked over to Simon approvingly.

WHAT THE JUDGES SAID:

Simon: 'I think there is potential with you, Liam. I'm just missing a bit of grit, a bit of emotion and actually a bit of fun, funnily enough.'

Cheryl: 'I like you; I think you're really cute. I think you've got charisma, you know you gave us that cheeky wink.'

Louis: '[to the other judges] I think this kid could do fantastic in the show.'

Simon: 'You know, a young guy, good-looking – people will like you, but there's something not... there's 20 per cent missing for me at the moment.'

Liam bravely told Simon: 'Give me another audition and I'll show you that I've got that extra 20 per cent.'

It paid off as all three judges gave Liam a 'yes' – he was going to Bootcamp! Mum Karen told the backstage camera: 'I'm so proud, I'm the proudest mum in the world!' Liam admitted: 'In the middle of the audition I was quite nervous but as soon as I started singing, I was alright.' He was determined to work hard so that Simon would be impressed by his next performance.

Only 150 out of the 182,000 people who applied made it to Bootcamp. For his first solo performance at Bootcamp Liam sang the Michael Bublé song 'Lost'. Louis told him: 'Very convincing, very professional and you're only fourteen.'

'Congratulations. You're a dark horse,' Simon added.

He also impressed Cheryl and Dannii Minogue, who was hearing him sing for the first time.

Liam told the backstage cameras: 'I've just got to do everything the best I can do – you know, just to get through – because the competition here is absolutely massive at the moment.'

For his second solo he sang Elton John's 'Your Song'. The judges couldn't give any feedback for this song, but after Liam left the stage Simon told the other judges, 'I like him.'

It was really difficult for the judges to choose the final 24 acts who would be making it to the Judges' Houses. When Simon addressed Liam and some of the other contestants who had been asked to line up on stage, he said: 'It was far from a unanimous decision. Whatever happens, you can walk away with your heads held high… it's bad news.'

Liam was devastated and started crying as he walked off stage. He wore his hat quite far down, which hid how upset he

8

was. When he saw the *X Factor* host Dermot O'Leary, Dermot gave him a pat on the back. Liam explained: 'I thought I'd done enough, I feel like something's been taken away from me.'

But Liam wasn't the only one upset – Simon was too because he had felt in his gut that Liam should make it through. He told the other judges: 'I really think we're making a mistake here.' Louis added: 'I liked him yesterday, I really liked him yesterday.' Simon concluded: 'I'm telling you I really think that this kid's got a shot... We want to get Liam back.

'I'd hate to see this guy go. It's the right decision, honestly. Promise you.'

A member of the production team went to get Liam, who was preparing to go home. As he walked back on stage and waited to hear what the judges wanted to say to him, he looked shell-shocked. Simon said: 'Liam, I don't often do this, but it was such a close call with you...'

Liam interrupted: 'I just want to say I really feel I can do this, I really do want to win this competition.'

Simon continued: 'I know you do. The other thing I wanted to say to you, Liam, is we've changed our minds.'

Liam couldn't believe it. Covering his face with his hands, he dropped to the floor. He couldn't stop smiling – his *X Factor* dreams weren't over yet! He knew that Simon had offered him a lifeline and he was determined to keep working hard to make sure he survived the next round. Now he was up against Alan Turner, Austin Drage, Eoghan Quigg, Mali-Michael McCalla and Scott Bruton in the Boys category. Only three singers would make it through to the live shows.

DID YOU KNOW?

When Liam rang his family back to tell them that he had made it through after all they didn't believe him. He ended up having to swear on his life to prove to them that he wasn't making it up!

In the weeks that followed Liam practised a lot but he had no idea where the boys were to be sent. He just had to wait for instructions at the airport with the other singers on the day they were due to fly out. Each category (Boys, Girls, Over-25s and Groups) was given an envelope revealing their secret location and for the boys that location was Barbados! Arriving at the luxury villa, they had to line up outside and then their mentor stepped out… It was Simon!

DID YOU KNOW?

While the boys were there they filmed a spoof *Baywatch*-type video that was really funny and well worth a watch on YouTube. Liam managed to get sunburnt feet, but the rest of him was okay.

Liam loved his time in Barbados, but he knew he had a job to do and as soon as he was told that Simon had chosen for him to sing Take That's 'A Million Love Songs', he made sure he knew the song inside out. He also picked out an audition outfit that would make him look like a pop star. He wore white trousers, a white T-shirt, a white unbuttoned shirt, sandals and accessorised with some dog tags.

Liam performed brilliantly, with Simon's helper Sinitta commenting that she loved him and she thought he had a really cute face. Liam also sang Enrique Iglesias's classic 'Hero'. He was happy with both of his performances and just hoped he'd done enough. However, he had to wait until the next day to find out his fate so he had a restless night. As Simon and

Sinitta sat and decided on the final three, there was a torrential storm. Sinitta was shocked by the singers that Simon had decided on because she would have chosen different ones and even Simon himself wasn't sure, admitting he would probably regret his decision.

The next day Liam told Dermot O'Leary: 'It's a numb feeling now, knowing that you've done all you can and there's nothing else you can do.

'As you get further and further through the competition you just think, I want this more, and I want this more and I want to get to the next stage... I got thrown out once at Bootcamp – that feeling after being thrown out, I was absolutely gutted. I don't want that to happen again.'

Facing Simon for his verdict, Liam looked petrified. Simon told him he looked like the perfect pop star, but it was still a 'no'. Liam tried to argue back, but it was no good. Simon had made his decision – he wanted Liam to go back to school and come back when he was older.

DID YOU KNOW?

Because Liam was only fourteen, his mum was allowed to travel to Barbados with him as his chaperone so she was able to comfort him when he didn't get through.

So Liam did just that. He went back to school but still dreamed of being a pop star. For a while he didn't do well in his subjects because his heart wasn't in it, but once he realised that he would need to pass his exams so he would have something to fall back on in the future he began to try harder. He ended up getting good results: an A*, two B's, six C's and a D.

Meanwhile Liam got as much experience as possible, singing at Party in the Park in Stourbridge with Ricky Loney, who had auditioned for *The X Factor* in 2008 and made the live shows in the 2009 series. He then performed with Same Difference at Wolverhampton's football stadium in front of nearly 30,000 people, singing during a Wolves vs Man U match and supported Peter Andre too. He did as many gigs as he could. For the Wolverhampton performance he sang 'Black and Gold' by Sam Sparro because the Wolverhampton Wanderers play in a black-and-gold coloured kit. Only a few people turned up for some of the gigs — for example, when he performed at The Sunshine Festival in Rhyl only ten people were in the audience, which must have been soul-destroying. His dad had driven for two hours to get Liam there and the £50 he was paid didn't cover much more than his petrol. Despite this, Liam still gave his best performance because he didn't want to let anyone down. Afterwards, he wondered if he should continue trying to be a singer because he was so upset.

DID YOU KNOW?

Liam is terrible at skateboarding. He told *Top of the Pops* magazine what happened when he tried the biggest ramp at a skatepark when he was sixteen. He confessed: 'I thought I'd be fine if I hurt myself, as I didn't have any gigs coming up. I went down the ramp, the skateboard flipped up and my head hit the floor.

'I got a massive graze and bruised my face, and when I got home my dad told me I had two gigs lined up — I had to perform them looking like that!'

Any money Liam ever made or was given as a gift he saved up and used to pay to get to London, as he was taking vocal lessons there. He knew that if he was to get to the *X Factor* live shows one day then he would need to have professional guidance to improve his voice and make it even stronger. By this time he had his own website and quite a few fans, who either lived locally or had seen him on TV. Looking back, he is so glad that Simon rejected him in 2008 because he was able to sit his GCSE exams and gain some experience. If Simon had said yes, then he would never have had the opportunity to be in One Direction.

TIME TO SHINE
– TAKE TWO

Liam had wanted to audition for *The X Factor* in 2009 but he couldn't because the minimum age had changed from fourteen to sixteen. He had missed out by a margin of just a few months. Instead he ended up enrolling in a sound technology course at Wolverhampton College and even contemplated doing an apprenticeship at the factory where his dad worked, building aeroplanes. Thankfully, he didn't give up and auditioned again in 2010.

> **DID YOU KNOW?**
> Even though Liam had been on the show before he wasn't treated any differently and still had to queue up for thirteen hours before his second *X Factor* audition.

Liam had the strongest audition out of all of the One Direction boys. Although he had faced Simon, Louis and Cheryl before, this time he had a new judge to impress: Australian singer-songwriter Natalie Imbruglia. The format of the audition had changed since he was last on the show. This time around he had to sing with 3,000 people in the audience, rather than just singing in front of the judges in a private room. His outfit was more grown up: a tight white T-shirt, dark blue jeans, big black boots and a black belt.

DID YOU KNOW?

When Liam auditioned in 2008, his shoes had a hole in them and he had borrowed his jeans!

Liam told the backstage cameras: 'I feel like today is my chance to prove to Simon that I have got what it takes. It would mean more than anything to get a "yes" off Simon today.'

Even though it had been a couple of years since Simon had seen Liam he still recognised him when he walked on stage. Liam even commented that he hadn't seen Simon Cowell in a while. For this audition he had chosen to sing 'Cry Me A River'. Cheryl mistakenly thought that he was going to sing the Justin Timberlake song but in fact he was going to sing the classic blues ballad of the same name, written by Arthur Hamilton and first made famous by Julie London in 1955. Liam was playing to his strengths and he knew that Simon liked the Blues, too, from past experience. He was also inspired to sing the song because a former girlfriend had cheated on him and he could empathise with its sentiment.

Liam started strongly and the audience were blown away. Before he could even finish, everyone took to their feet to applaud him, with even Simon and Natalie joining in. All the big performances that he had done since he was last on the show had made him even more confident than in 2008; he commanded the stage, and was boosted by the audience.

WHAT THE JUDGES SAID:

Cheryl: 'You've definitely got it, whatever it is, you've got it. And I thought your voice was really, really powerful.'

Natalie: 'That was really impressive, really, really impressive. I think other people in this competition should be a little bit worried about you. You're really good.'

Louis: 'I'm really glad that you came back. It was a brilliant, brilliant vocal and for 16 years, it was so confident, you totally delivered. [Looking at Simon] Simon, this is the guy you didn't put through!'

Simon: 'He wasn't quite ready when he came to my house two years ago but I said to him then, "Come back, two years' time and you're going to be a different person." I got it right!'

When it was time to vote Liam knew that he had to receive three yeses to make it through to Bootcamp so he could afford for one judge to say no. Thankfully he managed to get four yeses – quite an achievement. Simon said: 'Based on talent, absolutely incredible – one massive, fat, all-mighty yes!' and gave Liam two thumbs-up to show just how pleased he was.

Liam couldn't contain his excitement and as soon as he left the stage he was surrounded by his proud family, who gave him a massive hug. His mum told him: 'Oh my gosh, you were absolutely awesome!'

Dermot added: 'The boy becomes a man!'

Liam also went into the *X Factor* booth and told the cameras:

'I never expected in my wildest dreams for that to happen and to get that reaction – you know, it was so amazing! Simon stood up for me and that's just the most amazing thing in the world ever.'

DID YOU KNOW?

As Liam left with his family, he told them his face hurt because he couldn't stop smiling.

Next stop for Liam was Bootcamp, which was held at Wembley Arena over five days at the end of July 2010. Liam was one of only 211 acts who had made it. The first song he was asked to sing was Michael Jackson's 'Man In The Mirror'. He then had to showcase his dancing skills and for his final Bootcamp performance he had 40 songs to choose from. He picked 'Stop Crying Your Heart Out' by Oasis, which incidentally was the song Harry Styles chose to sing too. Liam told the backstage camera: 'I want to show Simon that I mean business and that I have what it takes. This is the moment I've been waiting for.'

Former Pussycat Doll judge Nicole Scherzinger and Louis Walsh thought Liam performed 'Stop Crying Your Heart Out' wonderfully but Simon didn't think the performance was as strong as Liam's first audition. He told the other judges: 'I like him but I think it was a little bit one dimensional.'

In some ways Liam would have agreed with Simon as he explained to the backstage cameras before he performed: 'Having such a good first audition, I mean, it's a brilliant bonus and I'm still buzzing now, my feet haven't touched the floor but it's also a negative because I've got to try and live back up to that. The difference is I had a whole year to work on that performance whereas I've only had, what, twenty-four hours to work on this one.'

> **DID YOU KNOW?**
> In rehearsals Liam had struggled to remember his lines and was advised that if his mind went blank he should try and carry on, rather than starting the song all over again. Thankfully he managed fine when he actually performed and felt relieved as he walked off stage.

At Bootcamp all the singers got on really well together. Liam and Niall even ended up sharing a hotel room. Niall had brought his guitar with him so he took it to the arena and would sing with Liam and some of the other contestants. To see videos of their jamming sessions, search on YouTube for John D'Ambrosio's channel. John failed to make the next round, but did well in *Britain's Got Talent* (2012). Liam first met Zayn in McDonald's and he thought Louis was shy until he got to know him.

At Bootcamp Liam got to know Cher Lloyd (she would end up finishing in fourth place in the series). Some newspapers suggested that they had dated but they were only ever friends. Liam explained to *X Magazine*: 'We made friends downstairs in the hotel at Bootcamp and all I said was, "Do you wanna come back to the room?" I know that sounds bad, but I just meant it in a totally innocent hanging out sense.'

Liam's mum Karen was even asked if the two were having a relationship. She told *new!* magazine: 'There's nothing in it. Liam has a connection with Cher because she's a similar age and they're from a similar part of the country. And he gave her a hug when she got through at Bootcamp, which was on film. It got blown out of proportion.'

Liam really thought he had done enough to make it to the 'Judges' Houses' round and so he was devastated when the judges called out the names of the boys who had made it through and his name wasn't called. He was going home... until he was offered a lifeline alongside four other soloists who had been rejected, too: Harry Styles, Louis Tomlinson, Zayn Malik and Niall Horan. Simon, Nicole and Louis wanted them to join together and create a group. The others were all up for it, but it took Liam a bit longer to agree – he wanted to make sure he was making the right decision. He had only ever really considered being a solo artist so the idea of being in a group was going to take time. In the end he couldn't help but say yes – after all, it was such a fantastic opportunity – and with the rest of the boys he had a shot at making the live shows as they had been offered a place at Judges' Houses.

DID YOU KNOW?

Although the first auditions hadn't been shown on TV at this point, by the time they were broadcast the general public had picked out Liam as the second favourite to win, with just Cher Lloyd in front of him. They were shocked when he got rejected, but excited when they found out it wasn't the end of Liam's *X Factor* journey. The Bootcamp episodes of *The X Factor* aired on Saturday, 2 and Sunday, 3 October 2010.

Liam might have had his reservations in the beginning but after the boys had spent some time together at Harry's home in Holmes Chapel, Cheshire and then flown to Marbella in Spain for Judges' Houses everything was great between them and they had all become good friends. They had bonded so much at Harry's home, getting up to all kinds of mischief. Harry's mum Anne had been having some work done so there was a tractor-type machine there and the boys decided to drive it when the workmen went home, knocking things down. Zayn also managed to set fire to half a sofa, too — which Anne can't have been happy about!

By the time they arrived at the airport the boys had also decided to call themselves One Direction, a name that Harry came up with. Zayn explained how the name came about to Hot 95.7FM Phoenix. He said: 'Basically we just came up with the idea to make loads of names up and it was one of the first names Harry came up with. He just texted it to us and we were like, "Yeah, I like that, it's cool."

'There were some really embarrassing ones that Liam came up with… What was the other one? USP — Unique Selling Point.'

Louis added: 'That is the WORST! Although to be fair, you have to be brave even to mention it in the first place. I think it came from his dad… Sorry, Geoff!'

Liam was so happy when Simon told them he was taking them through to the live shows — his dreams were finally coming true.

While the boys were on *The X Factor Live* shows they lived together with the other singers in a luxury house in Borehamwood, North London. Their favourite room was the chill-out room, which had a big couch, loads of beanbags, a table-tennis table, huge TV and a Wii. Liam also liked spending time in the music room, which had a jukebox and a piano. The boys' room was very crowded and Liam was often woken up when the others came to bed. He likes his sleep and needed to rest after a long day of rehearsing but the others didn't seem to need so much slumber and would stay up later.

Liam told the *Shropshire Star* at the time: 'It's different. If you don't get to see it and experience it first-hand, you wouldn't understand what it is like. It's so much fun. There is never a dull moment, and it is always loud in the house. That's usually probably coming from our band. Everyone has such a great time and it is surprising how well everybody gets on because at the end of the day it is a competition, but everybody gets on great.'

DID YOU KNOW?

While living in the house Liam admitted that in the following two years he would love to have a house in America, as well as one in London. He sees America as being his second home.

CHAPTER THREE

X FACTOR LIVE SHOWS, WEEKS ONE TO FIVE

WEEK 1 – NO. 1S

9 October 2010 was a monumental day for Liam, Zayn, Louis, Niall and Harry, and the other 11 acts picked at Judges' Houses. At the start of the show four wildcards were revealed, one for each judge. Simon Cowell's wildcard group were Diva Fever. Liam and the boys had been rehearsing for weeks but Zayn was struggling with his nerves. He was having problems coming in on time and thought that if it happened in the live show, he would ruin things for the others. Of course none of the boys wanted to be sent home in the first week. Thankfully, on the night Zayn did come in on time and the boys did a great version of 'Viva La Vida' by Coldplay.

WHO SANG WHAT:

Aiden Grimshaw – 'Mad World' by Tears For Fears

Belle Amie – 'Airplanes' by B.O.B

Cher Lloyd – 'Just Be Good To Me' by Beats International

23

Diva Fever – 'Sunny' by Bobby Hebb
FYD – 'Billionaire' by Travie McCoy feat. Bruno Mars
John Adeleye – 'One Sweet Day' by Mariah Carey and Boyz II Men
Katie Waissel – 'We Are The Champions' by Queen
Mary Byrne – 'It's A Man's Man's Man's World' by James Brown
Matt Cardle – 'When Love Takes Over' by David Guetta
Nicolo Festa – 'Just Dance' by Lady Gaga
One Direction – 'Viva La Vida' by Coldplay
Paije Richardson – 'Killing Me Softly With His Song' by The Fugees
Rebecca Ferguson – 'Teardrops' by Womack & Womack
Storm – 'We Built This City' by Starship
Treyc Cohen – 'One' by U2
Wagner – 'She Bangs' and 'Love Shack' medley by Ricky Martin and The B-52s

WHAT THE JUDGES THOUGHT:

Louis: 'Wow, guys, when I heard you were going to do Coldplay I thought it was a big, big risk! I love what you did with the song – you totally made it your own. I love that the band is gelling. Even though Simon's going to claim he put this band together, it was my idea originally, Simon. It was! Boys, I think potentially you could be the next big boy band but you have a lot of work to do. But Simon, I'm not sure about the styling. Did you have a stylist?'

Dannii: 'Guys, I don't know whose idea it was because I wasn't there, but you look like you fit together like you're the perfect band. That song was fantastic, and you did make it your own. I wasn't thinking of Coldplay then, it was the perfect pop band performance.'

Cheryl: 'I have to agree with Dannii, you look like you were meant to be together as a group. You look fantastic; you've got all the ingredients of the perfect pop band. I reckon the girls will be going crazy for you, but you need a little bit more time to develop as a group, that's all. Just a little bit more time.'

Simon: 'Regarding your role in putting the group together, Louis, we'll rewind the tapes on that one. You guys came together because your Bootcamp auditions weren't good enough but you were too good to throw away. We took a risk, and I've got to tell you, what was so impressive about that was when you started to screw up one of you at the end, Liam stepped in; you brought it back together. That's what bands do. Regarding the whole styling issue, Louis, I don't want to style this band because I don't know how to style a band like this. We asked the band to do whatever they wanted to do. I'm not going to interfere – they're going to do it their way. It was brilliant, guys!'

WHAT THE BOYS THOUGHT:

Liam and the boys were so happy that they weren't in the bottom two so they didn't need to worry about the sing-off. Now they could just look forward to the challenges of Week 2. Zayn told the backstage cameras: 'We came off the stage after our performance, we were all buzzing. I don't know how to describe what it was like because you will never understand what it was like until you've actually performed on the stage. It was just amazing!'

THE SING-OFF:

Nicolo Festa (from Dannii's Boys category) received the lowest vote so he automatically departed and became the first act to leave the show. The sing-off was between Katie (from Cheryl's

Girls category) and FYD (Simon's Groups category). Katie sang 'Don't Let Me Down' by The Beatles and FYD sang Rihanna's 'Please Don't Stop The Music'. Simon voted to save his own act, FYD, but the other judges all voted for Katie to stay. FYD became the second act to leave the show.

WEEK 2 – HEROES

On 16 October the remaining 14 acts had to sing songs from their musical heroes. One Direction chose to sing the Kelly Clarkson song, 'My Life Would Suck Without You'. It was an unusual choice for five teenage boys but considering Kelly won *American Idol*, it made perfect sense because they wanted to win *The X Factor*.

With just hours to go before the live show the boys had their sound check, but it didn't go well. When it was Harry's turn to sing, he found that he couldn't get the words out. He felt like he was going to be sick and the *X Factor* staff rushed him to see a doctor. It turned out that he wasn't suffering from an illness but that it was a bad case of stage fright. Thankfully, by the time it was the live show he had managed to control his nerves and could sing again.

WHO SANG WHAT:
Aiden Grimshaw – 'Jealous Guy' by John Lennon
Belle Amie – 'You Really Got Me' by The Kinks
Cher Lloyd – 'Hard Knock Life' by Jay-Z
Diva Fever – 'Gotta Go Home/Barbra Streisand' by Boney M
John Adeleye – 'A Song For You' by Donny Hathaway
Katie Waissel – 'I'd Rather Go Blind' by Etta James
Mary Byrne – 'You Don't Have To Say You Love Me' by Dusty Springfield

Matt Cardle – 'Just The Way You Are' by Bruno Mars
One Direction – 'My Life Would Suck Without You' by
Kelly Clarkson
Paije Richardson – 'If I Ain't Got You' by Alicia Keys
Rebecca Ferguson – 'Feeling Good' by Nina Simone
Storm Lee – 'Born To Run' by Bruce Springsteen
Treyc Cohen – 'Purple Rain' by Prince
Wagner – 'Help Yourself' by Tom Jones

WHAT THE JUDGES THOUGHT:

Louis: 'Well, One Direction, you seem to be having fun on stage. I like the fact that you've gelled already. Every schoolgirl up and down the country is gonna love this. My only problem, boys, is with your mentor Simon. Kelly Clarkson, a hero? Simon, why? It was a strange song. Boys, you are really, really good, but I think Simon could've picked a better song.'

Dannii: 'Boys, maybe that's your musical hero. I have to say that you're five heartthrobs. You look great together, and Harry, whatever nerves you have, I'm sure that your friends and you stick together. The true measure of a boy band like you will be is when you sing your big ballad, so I will be looking forward to hearing that.'

Cheryl: 'I can't even cope with how cute you are, seriously. I can't! I just want to go over and hug them, in a nice way. You're so sweet, I'm watching you the whole time just thinking, "This is adorable". But I want to be able to be saying, "Wow, this is the new big boy band!", and I think that'll come in time.'

Simon: 'Okay, well, that time has just come. Let me tell you, you are the most exciting pop band in the country today. I'm being serious. There is something absolutely right.'

WHAT THE BOYS THOUGHT:
Niall: 'I think our performance went well last night – we had a good song, the crowd got behind us.'

The boys were glad that Harry managed to perform with them but they weren't sure if they had done enough until Dermot O'Leary announced that they had got through to Week 3.

THE SING-OFF:
This week two acts were eliminated. The first to go was the act with the lowest votes: Storm Lee. Following this, the acts with the second and third lowest votes had to face the sing-off. Simon's girl group Belle Amie sang 'Big Girls Don't Cry' by Fergie and his wildcard group, Diva Fever, sang Gloria Gaynor's 'I Will Survive'. Louis, Dannii and Cheryl all voted to send home Diva Fever, meaning that Simon didn't have to choose between his two groups.

Storm Lee became the third act and Diva Fever became the fourth act to leave the show.

WEEK 3 – GUILTY PLEASURES
For the third show on 23 October the 12 remaining acts had to sing songs that were their guilty pleasures. The boys spent a week rehearsing one song, only to be told by Simon (with one day to go) that they needed to change to another one.

WHO SANG WHAT:
Aiden Grimshaw – 'Diamonds Are Forever' by
Shirley Bassey
Belle Amie – 'I'll Stand By You' by The Pretenders
Cher Lloyd – Mash up of 'No Diggity' by Blackstreet
and 'Shout' by Tears for Fears

John Adeleye – 'Zoom' by Fat Larry's Band
Katie Waissel – 'I Wan'na Be Like You' (The Monkey
Song) from *The Jungle Book*
Mary Byrne – 'I Who Have Nothing' by Shirley Bassey
Matt Cardle – '… Baby One More Time' by Britney
Spears
One Direction – 'Nobody Knows' by Pink!
Paije Richardson – 'Ain't Nobody' by Chaka Khan
Rebecca Ferguson – 'Why Don't You Do Right' by
Nora Lee King
Treyc Cohen – 'Whole Lotta Love' by Led Zeppelin
Wagner – Mash up of 'Spice Up Your Life' by the Spice
Girls and 'Livin' La Vida Loca' by Ricky Martin

WHAT THE JUDGES THOUGHT:

Louis: 'You just have to walk out on the stage, everybody's screaming – it's like five Justin Biebers! And Liam, brilliant lead vocal from you! This band, you're really getting your act together. I think you are the next big pop band.'

Dannii: 'Being a band, everybody wants to live that dream with you. And it seems like you're living the dream, and loving the dream, and you're letting everyone in on that with you. Another great performance! I'm not sure why Pink is a guilty pleasure, though.'

Cheryl: 'You know what, guys? Let me just put this out there: you are my guilty pleasure. When you watch the TV and you see all the hysteria you caused when you went out there this week, that's what you should do. That's what boy bands should be about. Whenever The Beatles went anywhere they caused that level of hysteria. You're finding your feet now, I'm looking forward to seeing you improve even more.'

Simon: 'With regards to the song, we chose a song, didn't work.

But the good thing about you, guys, is that there's no bleating on about excuses – "I can't do this, I can't do that". It's just a song. You grabbed hold of it within twenty-four hours, practised. And I've got to tell you, apart from it being a great performance, I thought vocally, you've really, really made some really huge improvements. It's been an absolute pleasure working with you lot.'

WHAT THE BOYS THOUGHT:
The boys found changing the song at the last minute quite stressful but they knew that Simon was right – the Pink song suited them better. Liam liked that it was a ballad because Dannii had wanted them to sing something slower and it showed the audience at home the wide variety of songs they could sing.

Harry told the backstage cameras: 'The comments were absolutely brilliant! For us to keep proceeding in the competition we have to, we have to get better every week.'

The boys also revealed that their top three guilty pleasure tracks are: John Travolta singing 'Grease Lightning', 'Tease Me' by Chaka Demus & Pliers and 'I'm Too Sexy' by Right Said Fred.

THE SING-OFF:
The two acts to receive the lowest votes were John Adeleye from Louis' Over-28s category and Treyc Cohen from Cheryl's Girls category. John chose to sing 'Because Of You' by Kelly Clarkson and Treyc picked 'One Night Only' from the musical, *Dream Girls*. Louis chose to save his act, John, but the other three judges picked Treyc.

John Adeleye became the fifth act to leave the show.

WEEK 4 – HALLOWEEN

On 30 October the final eleven acts had to sing a Halloween themed song. All the acts performed wearing scary costumes.

WHO SANG WHAT:

Aiden Grimshaw – 'Thriller' by Michael Jackson

Belle Amie – 'Venus' by Bananarama

Cher Lloyd – 'Stay' by Shakespears Sister

Katie Waissel – 'Bewitched' by Steve Lawrence

Mary Byrne – 'Could It Be Magic' by Barry Manilow

Matt Cardle – 'Bleeding Love' by Leona Lewis

One Direction – 'Total Eclipse Of The Heart' by Bonnie Tyler

Paije Richardson – 'Back to Black' by Amy Winehouse

Rebecca Ferguson – 'Wicked Game' by Chris Isaak

Treyc Cohen – 'Relight My Fire' by Take That

Wagner – 'O Fortuna/Bat Out of Hell' by Meat Loaf

WHAT THE JUDGES THOUGHT:

Louis: 'First, I was thinking, why were you picking this song? But it absolutely worked. I love the whole *Twilight*, vampire thing going in the background, and you definitely gel as a band. Everywhere I go, girls are saying, "You know One Direction, tell One Direction I love them!" I think there's definitely something great about you; you definitely gel as friends. I love the way you all sing. Simon, it's definitely working. I'm not sure what the song's got to do with Halloween but guys, you're brilliant – keep doing it!'

Dannii: 'Guys, like I've said before, you are a boy band doing exactly what a boy band should do. I'm looking at you and thinking the styling is even better than any other week. You make vampire hot – I want to come to your party!'

Cheryl: 'It doesn't matter where I go, somebody, an older woman, young women, kids, everybody mentions One Direction. I think you have a really long way to go in this competition.'

Simon: 'Once again, a great performance. What I really admire about you guys is I know people are under pressure when you go into a competition like this – you've got to remember you're 16, 17 years old, the way that you've conducted yourselves… Don't believe the hype, work hard, rehearse… Honestly, total pleasure working with you lot.'

WHAT THE BOYS THOUGHT:

Harry told the backstage cameras on the Sunday: 'Last night felt brilliant! We got a real chance to show off our vocals and hopefully the fans at home will vote and keep us in because we really don't want to go home now.'

Liam and the boys were really grateful they had been given a classic song to sing because they felt it would appeal to a wide spectrum of people and some of the songs they had sung previously had been less well known.

THE SING-OFF:

Cheryl's act Katie Waissel and Simon's girl group Belle Amie received the lowest number of votes so they had to take part in the sing-off. Katie chose to sing 'Trust In Me' by Etta James and Belle Amie picked Kelly Clarkson's 'Breakaway'. Simon and Louis voted to send Katie home, with Dannii and Cheryl voting to send Belle Amie home. Because it was a draw the decision was left to the public vote and since Belle Amie received the fewest votes they were sent home.

Belle Amie became the sixth act to leave the show.

WEEK 5 – AMERICAN ANTHEMS

The fifth week of *The X Factor* live shows saw the ten remaining acts sing American Anthems on 6 November. By this point the boys were dreaming about possibly winning the show and Simon was doing his utmost to help them on their way. Simon thought that 'Kids In America' was the perfect song for 1D and their version could be a hit single if it was ever released. After the boys' song was criticised by Louis Walsh because 'Kids In America' isn't strictly an American Anthem, Simon said: 'When you came out, it was like sunshine on a beautiful day, and I've said this before, and then "Louis the thundercloud" comes along and dribbles on everything that is happy... Taking all that rubbish to one side, because it was about the artist, it was about song title, that was without question your best performance by a mile.'

WHO SANG WHAT:

Aiden Grimshaw – 'Nothing Compares 2U' by Sinéad O'Connor

Cher Lloyd – 'Empire State Of Mind' by Jay-Z and Alicia Keys

Katie Waissel – 'Don't Speak' by No Doubt

Mary Byrne – 'There You'll Be' by Faith Hill

Matt Cardle – 'The First Time Ever I Saw Your Face' by Roberta Flack

One Direction – 'Kids In America' by Kim Wilde

Paije Richardson – Mash up of 'I'm A Believer' by The Monkees and 'Hey Ya!' by Outkast

Rebecca Ferguson – 'Make You Feel My Love' by Bob Dylan

Treyc Cohen – 'I Don't Want To Miss A Thing' by Aerosmith

Wagner – Mash up of 'Viva Las Vegas' and 'Wonder Of You' by Elvis Presley

WHAT THE JUDGES THOUGHT OF ONE DIRECTION'S PERFORMANCE:

Louis: 'What a brilliant way to end the show! Listen, everywhere I go there's hysteria. It's building on this band. You remind me a bit of Westlife, Take That, Boyzone… You could be the next big band. I loved everything about the performance, but Simon, *Simon*, one point! I've had to get my rulebook out. The theme is "American Anthems" – this wasn't even a hit in America! It's by Kim Wilde… from London – it's not an American anthem so you cheated. Your mentor has cheated.'

Dannii: 'It had the word "America" in it, and it had American cheerleaders and it was a great performance, guys. I don't think vocally it was the best of the night, but a great performance.'

Cheryl: 'That absolutely cheered me up and brightened up my night! I thoroughly enjoyed that performance. You are great kids – I love chatting to you backstage, you are just good lads. Nice lads. Great performance; good song choice. Cowell, I've got to give it to you, but it isn't American all the same.'

Simon: 'When you came out, it was like sunshine on a beautiful day, and I've said this before, and then "Louis the thunder-cloud" comes along and dribbles on everything that is happy. Taking all that rubbish to one side, because it was about the artist, it was about song title – that was without question your best performance by a mile.'

WHAT THE BOYS THOUGHT:

The boys found performing 'Kids In America' really fun. They liked having the cheerleaders with them and were very grateful to Brian Friedman, who had created the fantastic choreography. They loved having the opportunity to close the show, too.

In their video diary that week Liam said: 'On behalf of all of us you can say that's the most fun we've ever had on *The X Factor* stage. When we did "Viva La Vida" the first week that was great, but this week was so much fun.'

THE SING-OFF:

Katie Waissel and Treyc Cohen received the lowest number of votes and so they were in the sing-off (both acts were in Cheryl's Girls category). Katie chose to sing 'Please Don't Give Up On Me' by Solomon Burke and Treyc picked Toni Braxton's 'Unbreak My Heart'. Simon voted to send Treyc home, Cheryl controversially refused to vote, Dannii voted to send Katie home and Louis chose to send Treyc home. Cheryl had thought that Dermot would let the vote go to deadlock but this wasn't the case.

Because she had received two votes to go home, Treyc became the seventh act to leave the show.

CHAPTER FOUR

X FACTOR LIVE SHOWS, WEEKS SIX TO TEN

WEEK 6 – ELTON JOHN

On 13 November, the remaining nine acts had to sing Elton John songs. Liam, Zayn, Louis, Harry and Niall were a bit unsure at the beginning of the week when they were told the theme because they didn't know that many Elton John songs. In the end they decided to go for 'Something About The Way You Look Tonight'. Liam told the backstage cameras shortly before they went onstage: 'This has easily been our best week yet and we'd like to end it with a great performance tonight.'

WHO SANG WHAT:

Aiden Grimshaw – 'Rocket Man'
Cher Lloyd – Mash up of 'Sorry Seems To Be The Hardest Word' and 'Mockingbird' by Eminem
Katie Waissel – 'Saturday Night's Alright For Fighting'
Mary Byrne – 'Can You Feel The Love Tonight'

Matt Cardle – 'Goodbye Yellow Brick Road'
One Direction – 'Something About The Way You
Look Tonight'
Paije Richardson – 'Crocodile Rock'
Rebecca Ferguson – 'Candle In The Wind'
Wagner – Mash up of 'I'm Still Standing' and 'Circle
Of Life'

WHAT THE JUDGES THOUGHT OF ONE DIRECTION'S PERFORMANCE:

Louis: 'Well, boys, after that performance I think you're only going in one direction… and that direction is the final! I talked to you guys a lot yesterday and I really got to know you. I know that you're taking the whole thing really, really seriously and you know you're going to be the next big boy band and you've gelled as friends, and I've nothing but good to say about One Direction!'

Dannii: 'Guys, you are so consistent – it's scary! That song could have been really boring but it was great. That's what I would love to hear you sing at your concerts, which I'm sure you will be doing one day.'

[Crowd cheers]

Cheryl: 'Listen to that! That's what it's about… to hear that is the measure of what you've become so you definitely are heading in one direction.'

Simon: 'Guys, I want to say something okay, this is the first time in all the years of *X Factor* where I genuinely believe a group are going to win this competition. And you know what, I want to say this: what was so impressive, you've seen the girls and anything else, you've remained focused, you've been really nice to the crew, you're nice to the fans and most importantly, everything that happened tonight, from the choice of song to what they wore, it was all down to you. Guys, congratulations!'

WHAT THE BOYS THOUGHT:
Liam and the boys were blown away by the judges' comments. Having to sing out of their comfort zone had been a positive thing rather than a negative.

Louis told the official *X Factor* website: 'Last night was absolutely incredible, the crowd were amazing!' Zayn added: 'The competition's really, really heating up.'

THE SING-OFF:
Cheryl's act, Katie Waissel, and Danni's act, Aiden Grimshaw, received the lowest number of votes so they had to sing for survival. Aiden had been the favourite to win the whole show so the audience watching at home and in the studio were shocked. Katie chose to sing 'Save Me From Myself' by Christina Aguilera and Aiden picked Crowded House's 'Don't Dream It's Over'. Simon and Cheryl both voted to send Aiden home, with Dannii and Louis voting to send Katie home. It all came down to the public vote and because Aiden received the least amount of votes he became the eighth act to leave the show.

DID YOU KNOW?
Eighteen-year-old Aiden Grimshaw from Blackpool was one of the boys' closest friends on *The X Factor* and they were devastated when he was told he was going home. While Aiden and Katie prepared to sing for survival in the advertising break Louis tweeted: 'What a joke Wagner through and not Aiden!!! Aiden has to get through!!!!'

After the result he angrily tweeted: 'Not only was he

one of my best friends, he was one of the best singers in the competition, yet people who can't sing a note in tune are still here. Wow.'

Liam joined in: 'Aiden didn't deserve that.'

And the boys weren't the only ones to be upset and angry after Aiden's *X Factor* dream was over. Dannii Minogue tweeted: 'My utmost respect to Aiden. I have loved working with him on X Factor. TeamMinogue will miss him and I wish him the VERY BEST! Dx'

Liam and Louis were more concerned about Aiden going than attacking Wagner for surviving another week. Wagner was seen as a 'joke' singer by many people who thought Louis Walsh shouldn't have chosen him for live shows, but somehow he kept surviving each week as members of the public voted to keep him in. A few weeks earlier, Liam had told his local paper, the *Express & Star*: 'I think everyone deserves their place in their own little way in *X Factor* because it is not just a singing competition, otherwise it would be called something else. He brings different things to the show. Everyone has got a guilty pleasure for Wagner as well.'

WEEK 7 – THE BEATLES

The seventh week of *The X Factor* live shows took place on 20 November and saw the eight remaining acts singing songs by The Beatles. Liam told the show's official website shortly before their performance: 'I'm a massive fan of The Beatles and I'm really looking forward to tonight. Although it's an oldie, we're going to make the song we sing tonight feel current. It's a complicated performance for us, full of harmonies and ad-libs, but it's the sort of performance that I think you'd expect from a top boy band. We're feeling the pressure a bit, but if it all goes to plan, it'll be awesome!'

WHO SANG WHAT:

Cher Lloyd – 'Imagine' by John Lennon
Katie Waissel – 'Help!'
Mary Byrne – 'Something'
Matt Cardle – 'Come Together'
One Direction – 'All You Need Is Love'
Paije Richardson – 'Let It Be'
Rebecca Ferguson – 'Yesterday'
Wagner – Mash-up of 'Get Back', 'Hippy Hippy Shake' and 'Hey Jude'

WHAT THE JUDGES THOUGHT OF ONE DIRECTION'S PERFORMANCE:

Louis: 'Hey, One Direction, thank God for you guys! You lifted the whole energy in the studio. Good to see the Fab Five singing the Fab Four. The hysteria here has lifted your game – you are in it for the long haul, yes!'

Dannii: 'Guys, another fantastic performance! I've always given you good comments – I just have to say tonight you guys (Niall and Zayn) were struggling. I don't know if it was caught on camera, but you were struggling with the backing vocals. You didn't know if you were coming in or out. Don't let the other guys down – you have to work as a group.'

Cheryl: 'I could get into the whole, "I don't know why your mentor put you on a plain platform like that" but I won't because above everything else, that was another great performance from you guys.'

Simon: 'Who cares about the platform? Can I just say, guys, as always you worked hard, delivered a fantastic, unique version of the song and please, for anyone at home who saw what happened last week, please don't think these guys are safe. This lot [Louis, Dannii and Cheryl] do not want you to do well in the competition. I do… please vote.'

Cheryl had criticised the boys standing on a platform because earlier in the show Simon had criticised her decision to place Cher Lloyd on a staircase for her performance of 'Imagine'. It was all very petty.

WHAT THE BOYS THOUGHT:
Niall believed it was their best performance to date. Liam told the backstage cameras: 'Dannii gave us a bad comment but we're going to get bad comments so we've just got to take it on board and improve it next week.'

THE SING-OFF:
Cheryl's act, Katie Waissel, and Dannii's act, Paije Richardson, received the lowest number of votes so they had to sing for survival. Katie chose to sing 'Stay' by Shakespears Sister and Paije picked Sam Brown's 'Stop'. Dannii voted to send Katie home, with the other three judges all voting to send Paije home.

Paije became the ninth act to leave the show.

WEEK 8 – ROCK WEEK
On 27 November the theme was Rock and the remaining seven acts had to sing two rock-themed songs each. Having to sing two songs rather than one put all the acts under extra pressure, but especially 1D because they had to sort out harmonies. At the last minute everyone found out that two acts would be leaving the show instead of just one. The act that received the fewest votes would automatically go and then the second and third from the bottom would have to sing again.

WHO SANG WHAT:

Cher Lloyd – 'Girlfriend' by Avril Lavigne, 'Walk This Way' by Run DMC/Aerosmith

Katie Waissel – 'Sex On Fire' by Kings Of Leon, 'Everybody Hurts' by R.E.M.

Mary Byrne – 'All I Want Is You' by U2, 'Brass In Pocket' by The Pretenders

Matt Cardle – 'I Love Rock'n'Roll' by Joan Jett and the Blackhearts, 'Nights In White Satin' by Moody Blues

One Direction – 'Summer Of 69' by Bryan Adams, 'You Are So Beautiful' by Joe Cocker

Rebecca Ferguson – 'I Still Haven't Found What I'm Looking For' by U2, 'I Can't Get No Satisfaction' by Aretha Franklin

Wagner – 'Creep' by Radiohead, 'Addicted To Love' by Robert Palmer

WHAT THE JUDGES THOUGHT OF ONE DIRECTION'S PERFORMANCES:

Performance 1 – 'Summer Of 69'

Louis: 'Hey, boys, that absolutely worked! I love the choice of song, I love the vibe, the vitality you bring to the competition... The competition would not be the same without One Direction. I love the way that you've gelled as friends. I think you're the next big boy band.'

Dannii: 'You've clearly done lots of work and really stepped it up – I like that.'

Cheryl: 'We've got feet stamps going on, there's electricity in the room – it's fantastic! You just keep growing and growing, and getting better and better. I think there's a big future for you, congratulations.'

Simon: 'I had nothing to do with this song choice – Harry chose the song, great choice of song. Just remember next week is the semi-final. You've worked your butts off to get where you've got to – you've got to be there next week. Please pick up the phone.'

> **DID YOU KNOW?**
> 'Summer of 69' was the first song Harry ever performed with his band, White Eskimo.

Performance 2 – 'You Are So Beautiful'

Louis: 'Wow, boys! You've proven tonight you're not just another boy band – you're a brilliant, brilliant vocal group and you've proved that everybody in this group can sing. Which is incredible. I love the song; I love everything about it. I don't think it's a rock song, Simon, it's in the rules, but it is a brilliant song. It's not really a rock song, is it?'

Dannii: 'Guys, there's one word for that and that's stunning. Absolutely wonderful!'

Cheryl: 'It's great to see you having fun, and having all the dancers and all of that. I love that side of you, but I absolutely loved you standing and hearing you sing. It's what it's all about. You should be able to do everything and I think you've got a really bright future as a boy band, I really do.'

Simon: 'This was in some ways my favourite performance by you because it was beautifully sung and Zayn in particular, I can remember back at Bootcamp and I had to get you from the back because you were too embarrassed to dance, and I've seen how you've transformed, found your confidence and how the boys have looked after you. Genuinely, I am so proud of you tonight, congratulations.'

WHAT THE BOYS THOUGHT:

While the boys hoped they had done enough, they couldn't be sure. They ended up being the last act to be named by Dermot as having a guaranteed place in the semi-final. Louis confided in the *Doncaster Today* that before their name was called, he thought they wouldn't be safe. He said: 'All I remember thinking was that we needed to smash our "save me" song so that we could stay in the competition. We don't know from week to week if we are going to get through because there's been a lot of surprises.'

After the boys had left the stage Niall jumped high in the air 'like a kangaroo' according to Louis and the boys all celebrated with their families.

Louis added: 'The pressure is really on, we've not had a minute. We're constantly working and improving our vocals. We've been doing eighteen-hour days and have been in the studio until 2am so it's really tough.'

THE SING-OFF:

Katie Waissel received the fewest votes so she was automatically sent home. Louis' two acts, Wagner and Mary Byrne, were in the sing-off. Wagner chose to sing 'Unforgettable' by Nat King Cole and Mary picked Shirley Bassey's 'This Is My Life'. Wagner had had a great run but his time had come to a close. Louis, Dannii and Cheryl chose to send him home so Simon didn't have to vote, but if he had then he too would have sent Wagner home.

Wagner became the eleventh act to leave the show.

WEEK 9 – SEMI-FINAL

For the semi-final on 4 December the final five acts had to perform two songs. The first had to be a Club Classic and the second could be any song at all so long as it would cause people at home to pick up their phones and vote for them.

WHO SANG WHAT:

Cher Lloyd – 'Nothin' On You' by B.O.B, 'Love The Way You Lie' by Eminem

Mary Byrne – 'Never Can Say Goodbye' by Gloria Gaynor, 'The Way We Were' by Barbra Streisand

Matt Cardle – 'You've Got The Love' by Florence and the Machine, 'She's Always A Woman' by Fyfe Dangerfield

One Direction – 'Only Girl In The World' by Rihanna, 'Chasing Cars' by Snow Patrol

Rebecca Ferguson – 'Show Me Love' by Steve Angelo, 'Amazing Grace' (Susan Boyle version)

WHAT THE JUDGES THOUGHT OF ONE DIRECTION'S PERFORMANCES:

Performance 1 – 'Only Girl In The World'

Louis: 'Week after week, you're getting better and better, and you bring hysteria to the show. If there is any justice you will absolutely be in the final – you deserve to be in the final! I think you're the next big boy band and you know, guys, I love the way you've gelled. I know you're best friends and you've got something special.'

Dannii: 'Guys, I hope you never let us down because I really wanna see you guys as the next big boy band. I have to say, some weeks you come out and I think it's very samey. That one was brilliant, you really stepped it up for the semi-finals. Brilliant!'

Cheryl: 'Okay, first of all I'm gonna say I love you guys. This week, for me, I got to know you all a little bit better because your mentor wasn't here [Simon had been suffering with flu all week so Cheryl had stepped in]. I thoroughly enjoyed mentoring you, thank you for that opportunity, but that song for me was a little bit dangerous because it's so current, right now as Rihanna's record that you have to completely make it like it was never, ever written for her and I don't know if it quite worked for me but I don't think it makes a difference. I hope to see you in the final.'

Simon: 'Someone's being tactical [referring to Cheryl's comments]. I've got to tell you, guys, I know this is going to sound a little bit biased but I thought the song was absolutely perfect for you because it is exactly what I liked about them: they didn't take the safe option. They chose something completely different; they had the guts to do it. I thought you looked current, sounded current and standing by what Cheryl said, you guys are just fantastic to work with. Can I just say, you hear all the applause and people at home might think you're safe but nobody is safe in this competition and I would urge anyone, please, if they want to see these boys in the final, please pick up the phone and vote for them because they deserve it.'

Performance 2 – Chasing Cars

Louis: 'Liam, Zayn, Niall, Harry and Louis, I know your names! Guys, there's something about this band – you've definitely got something special. I think you're the next big boy band, but I said that last week. I loved the song choice, I loved the whole styling, I love the fact that you're really good friends. There's a great vibe about you. If there's any justice all the young kids will pick up their phones and they're going to vote One Direction – you deserve it!'

Dannii: 'Guys, you've got through a really tough week and that was such a classy, classy performance! You've just grown up in front of our eyes and we've never, ever had such a good band on *The X Factor* – so proud to see you perform on this show.'

Cheryl: 'I know me, personally, all the crew, all the staff… everybody has grown so fond of you guys over the last few weeks. This week I was so impressed. You didn't have Zayn, Simon wasn't around, you showed a real level of maturity and you really deserve a place in the final.'

Simon: 'Guys, Tim who's been working with you all week told me that you made a decision this morning to get in at eight in the morning so you could give yourselves more rehearsal time and that's what it's all about. It's not about excuses, it's about having that great work ethic, picking yourselves up after what was a very tough week, and I said this before, I genuinely mean this: I am proud of you as people, as much as I am artists. That was a great performance, good for you!'

WHAT THE BOYS THOUGHT:

The boys were happy with their performances and just hoped they had done enough. They were pleased that Simon had enjoyed their two performances and hoped that their fans at home would vote – they wanted to be in the final so much!

THE SING-OFF

Cheryl's act, Cher Lloyd, and Louis' act, Mary Byrne, were in the bottom two and had to sing for a place in the final. Cher chose to sing Britney Spears' 'Everytime' and Mary picked the song she had sung in Week 1, 'It's a Man's Man's Man's World' by James Brown. Louis voted to save Mary, but the other three judges voted for Cher to stay.

Mary became the thirteenth person to leave the show.

WEEK 10 – THE FINAL

The final took place on 11 and 12 December. Liam finished the boys' last ever *X Factor* video diary by saying: 'We just really want to thank everybody for all the support we've had so far throughout the competition and we just can't believe it, it's unreal. Thank you so much to everybody who's been voting for us and please keep voting.'

SATURDAY – WHO SANG WHAT:

Cher Lloyd – Mash up of '369' by Cupid ft B.o.B and 'Get Your Freak On' by Missy Elliott
Matt Cardle – 'Here With Me' by Dido
One Direction – 'Your Song' by Elton John
Rebecca Ferguson – 'Like A Star' by Corinne Bailey Rae

WHAT THE JUDGES THOUGHT OF ONE DIRECTION'S PERFORMANCE:

Louis: 'Hey, One Direction, you're in the final! I hope you're here tomorrow night. It's amazing how five guys have gelled so well. I know you're all best friends. I've never seen a band cause so much hysteria so early in their career. I definitely think that you've got an amazing future. Niall, everybody in Ireland must vote for Niall, yes!'

Dannii: 'Guys, you have worked so hard in this competition. You were thrown together, you deserve to be here and I'd love to see you in the final tomorrow.'

Cheryl: 'You know what? I have thoroughly enjoyed watching you guys growing every week, having the most amount of fun possible and I think that you deserve to be standing on that stage tomorrow night.'

Simon: 'I would just like to say after hearing the first two performances tonight, Matt and Rebecca, they were so good, my heart was sinking. And then you came up on stage, you've got to remember that you're sixteen, seventeen years old, and each of you proved that you should be there as individual singers: you gave it 1,000 per cent. It's been an absolute pleasure working with you. I really hope people bother to pick up the phone to put you through tomorrow because you deserve to be there.'

DUETS – WHO SANG WHAT:

Cher Lloyd – Mash up of 'Where Is The Love' and 'I Gotta Feeling' with Will.i.am
Matt Cardle – 'Unfaithful' with Rihanna
One Direction – 'She's The One' with Robbie Williams
Rebecca Ferguson – 'Beautiful' with Christina Aguilera

THE RESULT:

Cher Lloyd received the fewest number of votes so she became the thirteenth act to leave *The X Factor* 2010.

SUNDAY – WHO SANG WHAT:

Matt Cardle sang 'Firework' by Katy Perry
One Direction sang 'Torn' by Natalie Imbruglia
Rebecca Ferguson sang 'Sweet Dreams' by Eurythmics

WHAT THE JUDGES THOUGHT OF ONE DIRECTION'S PERFORMANCE:

Louis: 'One Direction, you're in the final, you could be the first band to win *The X Factor* – it's up to the public at home. But you've got brilliant chemistry, I love the harmonies, I love the song choice and we've got five new pop stars!'
Dannii: 'Guys, you've done all the right things to make your place here in the final. That was a fantastic performance!

Whatever happens tonight I'm sure you guys are going to go on and release records and be the next big band.'

Cheryl: 'It's been so lovely to watch you guys from your first audition. To think that was only a few months ago. I really believe that you've got a massive future ahead of you and I wanna say thank you for being such lovely guys to be around. It's been great getting to know you and good luck with the show tonight.'

Simon: 'Let's be clear. Anyone who comes into this final has got a great chance of bettering their future but this is a competition and in terms of the competition, in terms of who's worked the hardest, who I think deserves to win based on the future of something we haven't seen before, I would love to hear your names read out at the end of the competition. Because I think you deserve it.'

THE RESULT:

Poor Liam, Louis, Harry, Niall and Zayn were gutted when Dermot announced that they had finished in third place. They had wanted to win so badly. The winner was Matt Cardle and Rebecca Ferguson was the runner-up.

DID YOU KNOW?

One artist who inspires Liam is Jay-Z. Liam would love to work with him one day. He admitted to MTV: 'I would love to do a hip-hop collaboration with Jay-Z… I don't know how to talk to him, though. I think he's wicked. I love Jay-Z. It upsets me that we're not cool enough, but I wish we could.'

Liam only got a few days off during *The X Factor* live shows but he made sure he used his time off wisely, travelling home to see his family and friends. He chatted to his local paper, the *Express & Star*, about one trip: 'It was my sister Ruth's 20th birthday so I came back to Wolverhampton and spent some time with my family. Not many people noticed me; no one knew I was going to be there. We went out for a meal at Frankie & Benny's at Merry Hill. More people noticed me there and lots of people came over for autographs and photographs.'

One of Liam's *X Factor* highlights was performing in Wolverhampton on the week of the final. He loved singing to thousands of people in his home city and enjoyed seeing all the banners supporting 1D. In One Direction's last-ever video diary for *The X Factor* he said: 'Wolverhampton was absolutely awesome, the crowd were absolutely amazing – 5,000 people there waiting for us and we went on stage and did three songs and it was the best gig any of us had ever done.

'We just really want to thank everybody for all the support we've had so far throughout the competition and we just can't believe it, it's unreal. Thank you so much to everybody who's been voting for us and please keep voting.'

DID YOU KNOW?

When they started out the boys had certain things they liked to do before going on stage. They would get into a huddle, wish each other good luck and share some private jokes. They would drink water, Red Bull and Niall used to have some lemon and ginger tea. Liam would do a few press-ups to focus himself, Harry would change his underpants and Niall would change his socks.

CHAPTER FIVE

SINGING TO MILLIONS

Although the boys only managed to finish the show in third place they still received a record deal from Simon Cowell's label and set about becoming the huge stars they are today. It's amazing that the boys wouldn't have become a group if not for *The X Factor* judges putting them together at Bootcamp. Whenever Liam is asked the best thing about being on *The X Factor*, he says it was meeting Harry, Zayn, Louis and Niall. He couldn't imagine life without them.

Along with the other acts, the boys released a charity single during their time on *The X Factor*. It was a cover of David Bowie's 'Heroes' and the money raised went to the Help for Heroes charity. Liam and the boys visited Headley Court Military Rehabilitation Centre to meet some recovering soldiers and now understand a bit more about what they go through once they return to the UK. The single was a big hit and was No. 1 in the UK charts.

When they filmed the video the singers were joined in the studio by some of the people Help for Heroes have assisted. Liam told a reporter from the *Sun*: 'I can't believe some of the people who fight out there are younger than me. It's so shocking that people our age can come back from places like Afghanistan disabled forever. We're all really active in the band – we play football and work out all the time. The thought of not being able to do that is horrible.'

Niall added: 'It really puts things into perspective. We all complained about having to get up early and do this video shoot this morning – I feel so bad about that now. You don't realise how lucky you are. We're doing a huge TV show and other people have really, really tough jobs.'

The boys loved filming the video and performing the track on *The X Factor* live show a few days later. When it went to No. 1 Zayn told Radio 1 host Reggie Yates: 'It was pretty crazy when we were told we got to No. 1. Because it's for such a good cause and something we're all really proud about, that makes it so much better.'

During his time on *The X Factor* Liam managed to hurt himself on a rare night out when he went with the boys and fellow contestants Cher Lloyd and Mary Byrne to see Tinie Tempah perform at Koko in Camden, North London. When they were called onto the stage, he fell over and twisted his ankle. Though he pretended he was fine, afterwards he had to be helped into a car. Liam has had quite a few scrapes since joining One Direction and in May 2012 he broke his toe. He admitted on *Good Morning America*: 'I dropped a MacBook Pro on it, which is not a very exciting story at all.'

In December 2012 he was injured when the boys were mobbed by fans at Heathrow Airport car park on arriving back in London from New York. He later tweeted a photo of his injury with the comment: 'The awkward moment when a girl gives you a Chinese burn in the airport.

'My scratch is that bad I think I might just have to cut my arm off.'

There had been so many excited fans there, all desperate to get close to the boys, that their security team had struggled to keep them safe. It had actually been quite scary for Liam, Harry, Niall, Zayn and Louis.

DID YOU KNOW?

The boys still find it strange that they are famous. Liam told *Glamour* magazine: 'I don't think it's ever something we'll get fully used to. We kind of try to stay under the radar and not tweet where we are. Yesterday, me and Niall went out shopping in Amsterdam. And literally every single shop we went into, they had to close the shop because there were so many people outside. Some girl tried to pull my hair out. It's quite mad!'

One day Niall managed to scare fans by posting a photo of Liam with his face heavily bandaged on Twitter with the message: 'Wishin you a speedy recovery.' Fans thought that Liam had seriously injured himself as he looked really sad and his left eye was covered in a dressing. They started tweeting both Niall and Liam to ask what had happened. One fan wrote 'WHAT HAPPEND TO LIAM?!?!?!?! WHY DOES HE HAVE BANDAGES ON HIS FACE?!?!' and another fan asked him directly: 'What happened to your beautiful face? Why is it all bandaged up?'

Once fans realised it was just a hoax they found it funny and tweeted messages like: 'And @NiallOfficial stop wrapping @Real_Liam_Payne up in bandages. I almost had a heart attack looking at that this morning. Ya crazy kids' and '#ThingsYouShouldntDo Post a picture of Liam Payne in bandages and expect people to not freak out. Lol I'm cracking up.'

As well as being accident-prone Liam is quite clumsy and has tripped over his own feet when he's made his way on stage before and fell off a chair during an interview. Thankfully, he has never fallen over at a music awards ceremony. On 14 October 2012, Liam tweeted: 'Gott in yeaterday spilt a fulllllllllllll! Tub of pasta on the floor, stupid stupidd stupidddddd boy smelly pasta house.'

Liam and the boys might be great friends, but naturally they argue sometimes. They are never jealous of each other, though, even if the press tries to stir up trouble. In the beginning the press said that Louis, Zayn and Niall were jealous of Liam and Harry because they were the most popular members of the band but that wasn't true. The boys each have millions of devoted fans and the most popular member changes depending on which country they are visiting. When the boys were on *The X Factor* people read too much into interviews their families did, and came to the conclusion that there were jealousy issues. One such occasion was when Liam's mum Karen told *Heat* magazine: 'Liam has a very strong following. I can't speak for the other boys, I don't know about their solo careers, but Liam gigged all over the country so he has both options open, really.'

Niall's older brother Greg decided to set the record straight by speaking to a journalist from his local paper, the *Herald*. He said: 'It's absolute nonsense. The boys all get on really well together. They instantly bonded and have become the best of friends. I'm so proud of Niall – he is getting on great. He rang a few times during the week, but I don't want to talk to him because I just miss him so much. He is loving every second of the experience and the lads are all fantastic… they have a huge amount of respect for each other. They have gelled so well that it's like they have already known each other for ten years.'

The boys themselves spoke to Digital Spy in December 2010 about their close friendships and the little arguments they have. Louis admitted: 'Because we're around each other so often it's like arguing with your siblings. You fall out with them, go away and have a bit of a paddy, then come back and get over it.'

Liam added: 'I think every band has arguments but the funny thing is you just get over them really quickly. They last about five minutes. You just get over it because you know we're all going for the same thing so you just put your differences aside and get on with it.'

DID YOU KNOW?

Liam finds being mad at Louis impossible because Louis has the ability to make him laugh, no matter what. They have a good relationship because whenever Louis wants to be silly and mess around, Liam will normally join in.

In a separate interview with the *Shropshire Star* Liam admitted: 'The dynamic of our band is that there are loud people and there are quiet people, and there are people in between – I would say I am probably one of the in-between people and one of the quiet people. But we all get on so well, it's unbelievable. Everyone is just so happy… we just have a laugh 24/7.'

He thinks it's funny when they sometimes finish each other's sentences now – they just know what the other is going to say in interviews. They really are the best of friends and are like brothers. All five are down-to-earth and there isn't one person in the group who has a big ego. They are just

the same five lads as they were in the beginning when they
met at *X Factor* Bootcamp.

Liam loves his time on the road with the boys and the
pranks they play on each other in their tour van, at photo
shoots and while filming their videos or documentaries.
During an outside photo shoot Liam ended up getting a real
soaking, courtesy of Louis. He revealed to the *Shropshire Star*:
'We were playing football outside and the football went into
the pond. I went to get the football out of the pond and one
of the boys pushed me in.

'I think it was Louis – but it meant I got free clothes because
they didn't want the clothes back. I'm glad he pushed me in. I
got some nice free jeans out of it.'

The boys also wrestle their security team, which tires them
out because Paul Higgins and the rest of the security team are
big guys. Most of the time Paul's team wins but occasionally
1D manage to get them in a headlock and win. The boys have
a great relationship with their security team and think of them
as being like older brothers or father figures. They enjoy
keeping them on their toes and trying to slip away from them
sometimes.

When Liam was bored waiting at a studio one day he
decided to have some fun with Harry. They found a huge
cardboard box and hid Harry inside. Liam got the paparazzi
to guess who was hiding inside, the only clue being Harry's
hand, which was popping up through a gap. After they had
guessed, Liam then did the big reveal, with himself and Harry
laughing loads.

In an interview with *Teen Vogue* Louis talked about another
incident, saying: 'There's quite a lot of waiting around so we
often find the need to be a little mischievous. Like today, for
example, Liam and I managed to get on the roof of [the photo-

graphy studio], and we were hiding from everyone. We just try to keep ourselves entertained.'

> **DID YOU KNOW?**
>
> Liam thinks that Louis gets away with a lot of stuff that he, Harry, Niall and Zayn couldn't get away with, so if he could swap places with any member of 1D for a day then he would pick Louis.

In June 2012 Liam, Zayn, Louis and Niall decided to pour water down Harry's trousers when he fell asleep in their dressing room so it would look like he had wet himself. Poor Harry must have had a fright when he woke up!

Getting used to the paparazzi following him was hard at first because Liam is naturally a private person and wants to be able to get on with life without being followed 24/7. He now tries to sneak out of back doors wherever he can to avoid being surrounded when he leaves restaurants and stores. He told the *Shropshire Star*: 'We get chased by paparazzi... there will be about eight photographers there, just taking photos of you walking down the street. It's very, very weird. It's hard to get used to, but it's cool.'

> **DID YOU KNOW?**
>
> During an interview with MTV Niall was asked which member of the group he would like with him in a fight. He pointed at Liam and said, 'Liam. One man I wouldn't like to pass in a dark alley, he has got serious Hulk vibes going on.' Harry seemed to agree, saying: 'Yeah, when he gets angry, but sometimes his anger takes over too much.' The boys love joking around in interviews!

CHAPTER SIX

UP ALL NIGHT

The boys' first album was *Up All Night*, which was released in Ireland on 18 November 2011 and on 21 November in the UK. It charted at No. 1 in Ireland and No. 2 in the UK. On 13 March 2013 it was released in America and charted at No. 1. It was also No. 1 in Australia, Canada, Croatia, Italy, Mexico, New Zealand and Sweden.

UP ALL NIGHT TRACK LISTING:

1. 'What Makes You Beautiful'
2. 'Gotta Be You'
3. 'One Thing'
4. 'More Than This'
5. 'Up All Night'
6. 'I Wish'
7. 'Tell Me a Lie'

8. 'Taken'
9. 'I Want'
10. 'Everything About You'
11. 'Save You Tonight'
12. 'Stole My Heart'
Limited edition – Yearbook
13. 'Stand Up'
14. 'Moments'

Liam has just over seven minutes of solos on the album, slightly less than Harry but more than Niall, Zayn and Louis. He sings the first solo in all but two of the album's tracks. His favourite songs on the album are 'I Want', which was written by McFly's Tom Fletcher and 'One Thing', which was written by Savan Kotecha, Carl Falk and Rami Yacoub.

Carl Falk revealed to Examiner.com why Liam starts 13 out of the 15 tracks. He said: 'Liam's the one who starts the songs because he's got a deep voice, and most of the songs start with a lower register. It's natural for him to do that smooth, dark voice. It's the perfect way to start a song. And he's also got a really good falsetto, which has been useful for a lot of the new songs.'

DID YOU KNOW?

'One Thing' was originally two songs but the songwriters decided to take the chorus from one song, and the verses from the other to create 'One Thing'. It is Carl Falk's favourite track on the album – he likes it even more than their first single, 'What Makes You Beautiful'.

On Wednesday, 1 August 2012 Liam and the boys were presented with special plaques from their record company,

Syco, as they had achieved 12 million sales in less than a year. It was an incredible achievement for the boys who had worked so hard promoting *Up All Night* around the world.

Liam said at the time: 'We are obviously ecstatic and incredibly humbled by our award. We have an incredible team of people around us who have helped us achieve this, and above all, we would like to thank our fans. We owe all our success to them.'

No matter how many plaques and awards the boys win they will never become big-headed and insist they will always remember that they owe everything to their fans. Liam told the *Daily Star*: 'Our video for our new single ['One Thing'] was filmed in London. We're not divas, we've got no interest in jetting off to the Caribbean just to shoot a video.'

Harry agreed, saying: 'We're normal guys. We're not lads who went to stage school and we have our feet on the ground.'

For Liam the hardest song to sing on the album is 'Moments' because of how high he has to sing. All the boys find singing high difficult on different tracks – for Niall and Harry, it is 'What Makes You Beautiful', for Louis it is 'Save You Tonight', for Zayn it is both 'Save You Tonight' and 'Tell Me A Lie'.

DID YOU KNOW?

Because Liam is the most mature member of 1D he has been given the nickname 'Daddy Directioner'.

DID YOU KNOW?

When Liam was given the opportunity to be a Hits Radio DJ for a day he chose the following songs for his playlist: 'One Thing', 'I Want' and 'What Makes You Beautiful', 'Lego House' by Ed Sheeran, 'Dedication To My Ex (Miss

That)' by Lloyd, 'Don't Hold Your Breath' by Nicole Scherzinger and 'Cry Me A River' by Michael Bublé. In fact Michael Bublé considers Liam to be one of his friends and he gets on really well with Niall too. He told the *Irish Sun*: 'We talk all the time. What's so great about them is, and this is probably to do with where they grew up, but fame won't change those guys because they're just being themselves… they're just nice, young guys having a blast.'

CHAPTER SEVEN

FINDING HOME

Liam knew as soon as he signed 1D's record deal contract with the other boys that he would have to leave Wolverhampton and move to London. It was going to be tough saying goodbye to his family and friends but he had always known that London was the place where he had to live if he wanted to be a singer because of the recording studios and TV studios in the capital. Joining 1D was his first proper job as his only previous earning experience was selling sweets to his friends in school to make a bit of pocket money.

He still misses his home city loads, telling the *Sunday Life*: 'We've hardly been back at all and I do miss Wolverhampton.

'I really like going into the town centre and shopping, and doing things like sitting on the sofa, watching *Friends*. I'd even like to go back to school for a day.'

Liam started out living with the other boys in a luxury apartment in Princess Park Manor, Friern Barnet, but eventually started looking to move into his own place. In July 2012 he posted a photo on Instagram of himself and Danielle Peazer, his girlfriend at the time, holding hands with the caption: 'i'm her's and she's mine forever. {big news coming up} :).'

Many fans mistakenly thought this meant they were getting engaged but in fact it was that they were going to be moving in together. Liam later used Twitter to clear things up, tweeting a photo of some roses and the message: 'Danielle loves roses, so she was so happy when i got them for her! I am young, i know.

'But i love this woman, she is the one i want to be with in the future. Danielle is the one for me, i am sure. And please do not hate, if you love me. You all were excited about the "big news" right? Well, me and Danielle are moving in together and we are going to take the next step in our relationship.

'I try to keep my private life private from publicity but it's hard sometimes. I read all your comments on my last picture and i'll just say that last night was the best night of my life, i know what really matters: love! Thank you for showing so much love and respect. I love you all, have a nice day! Oh and follow Danielle.'

After they had moved in together Liam told the *Sun*: 'I can't have it too messy or she'll have a go at me. We haven't been there long. My girlfriend's there alone most of the time. It's just a base, really.'

He thinks he is much tidier and cleaner than Harry and Louis.

DID YOU KNOW?

Liam enjoys singing in the shower, especially songs by Irish band The Script. He has a bust of Iron Man in his house and keeps lots of mementos that fans have sent him. If he could have any superpower, he would choose to be invisible and if he could be any superhero, he would struggle to pick between Batman and Iron Man because he likes them both so much.

Liam loves meeting fans but he wants privacy when he is at home. He kindly asked fans to respect his wishes in two tweets that he sent in July 2012. In them he wrote: 'hi i just wanna say i love you guys and all but having strangers knock on my door and notes pushed through at 11 pm can be a little bit scary.

'i know you guys would feel the same about people knocking on your door you don't know so please don't come to my address much love liamxx'

CHAPTER EIGHT

GIRLS

Liam was ten or eleven when he had his first kiss and the first girl he ever sent a Valentine's Day card to was called Charnelle. He used to practise kissing on the back of his hand when he was at school. He doesn't use chat-up lines and likes girls who have nice eyes (especially if they're blue). He told 101.5 Jamz/Phoenix: 'All of us lads have different tastes. My and Niall's tastes are quite similar. We like shy girls who aren't too in your face. They're cute... nice smile, good sense of humour, just fun people.'

DID YOU KNOW?
When Liam was still at primary school he dated a friend of his sister's. He was nine and she was eleven, so it was quite a big age gap.

For his first ever date Liam went to the cinema and they went out for something to eat. Harry also watched a film on his first date – he can't remember what it was, but he can remember that they watched it at his house rather than going out.

Liam has never been good at reading the signals and when he was at school, he would mistakenly think that girls fancied him when they didn't at all. He dated a girl called Shannon Murphy but their relationship ended after *The X Factor* – they just didn't have the chance to see each other much. She had long brown hair and was very pretty. They went to their prom together, with Liam looking extremely handsome in a suit and Shannon wearing a floor-length purple gown. They still keep in touch now and there is no animosity.

Back in November 2010 when the boys were still on *The X Factor* one newspaper claimed that Liam had banned Zayn, Niall and Harry from dating during the show so they could focus on the music (Louis was already dating someone). It was all lies as Louis explained to *X Magazine*: 'Absolute tosh, the entire thing! Liam wouldn't be able to slap a girl ban on us if he tried.'

Liam added: 'This is the first I've heard of it. Am I supposed to have slapped a girl ban on myself too? That would just be stupid.'

Liam is a pretty romantic kind of guy and to show his love for someone, he would like to whisk them off for a romantic holiday. All the boys know how to treat girls well and their top three romantic songs are 'Make You Feel My Love' by Adele, 'Don't Want To Miss A Thing' by Aerosmith and 'The Way Love Goes' by Lemar. Liam's personal favourite is 'End of May' by Michael Bublé.

Liam's ex girlfriend was dancer Danielle Peazer. They met when Liam was on *The X Factor* as Danielle was one of the

backing dancers and started dating in 2010. In September/
October 2012, they split up briefly, got back together at
Christmas and then split up again in April/May 2013. The media
reported that it was because of their hectic work schedules. We
will have to wait and see if they get back together one day.

When Liam and Danielle split for the first time he told the
Sun: 'Danielle is great, I really hope we can still be friends. I
bought her a car for her birthday, but she really isn't fussed by
money or fame.'

The car Liam bought Danielle was an Audi TT, rumoured to
have cost £50,000 (approx. $76,310 dollars). Louis also bought
his girlfriend Eleanor a car for her birthday, a Mini One D. The
boys are certainly generous with their money.

DID YOU KNOW?

It was Harry who got Liam and Danielle together in the
first place. Liam revealed to i93 Dallas: 'This has never
been told before, but when I actually got with my
girlfriend, Harry was the boy that set us up.

'Also, Louis and Eleanor as well, was also Harry. Harry's
the magic match-up man. He's like Hitch, he can do it for
everyone else – he's a lonely old man!'

It is hard for all the boys when girls they are dating (or girls
they are photographed with, simply chatting to them) receive
hateful tweets from jealous fans. The majority of fans are fine
when Liam and the boys date but it is just a small minority
who take things too far. Liam tried to defend Danielle
numerous times but the abuse didn't stop. He tweeted:
'#SometimesIHateTwitter when it becomes a place to abuse
people who uve never met never did anything to you but you
still choose to be cruel.'

In an interview with *Now Magazine* he said: 'Twitter twists things a bit. People have a false sense of confidence behind a keyboard.

'Some of the things they say I just can't believe. I think, "How can you say that? You wouldn't be able to say that to someone on the street, so why say it now?" But it's one of those things.'

When Danielle tweeted a supportive message to Harry's mum Anne after she received abuse, Danielle received nasty messages back. Anne had tweeted that a percentage of One Direction fans were just weird and all Danielle had tweeted in response was 'never mind those people'.

Anne received a message back from a fan, stating: 'friendly reminder your son wouldn't be doing what he loves if it wasn't for us 'weird' people.'

She replied: 'I was referring to the deliberately inappropriate comments. I'm sure they'd manage without them.'

Another fan tweeted to Danielle: 'So you don't like us and u think we're weird? Wow.'

Danielle couldn't understand why they were being nasty to Anne and herself, tweeting: 'It's ok to not like rude people, I didn't say anything wrong.

'I don't quite understand why I get abuse for not liking rude people. That's just crazy. If you are kind to me I'll be kind to you.'

Liam was horrified in March 2013 when he read messages some fans had posted after he had shared a photo of his and

Danielle's new pet, a Siberian Husky puppy, with the message: 'Everybody meet mine and @daniellepeazer new dog Loki :)'

The majority of messages were positive, saying how cute Loki was, but some fans even threatened to kill the puppy. One 'fan' tweeted: 'The dog is not going to see tomorrow if i can help it... U were supposed to come back for me liam.' They also used the hashtag #dieloki and discussed whether they would shoot or stab the dog – it was horrifying to read their messages. The true fans who read the messages hit back, asking, 'Where are their parents and do they know they've raised little psychopaths?'

DID YOU KNOW?

When Tom Hiddleston picked up the Best Villain award at the MTV Movie Awards for playing Loki in *The Avengers* he mentioned Liam's dog in his acceptance speech. He said: 'I'd just like to thank Liam Payne from One Direction, who I believe named his dog Loki.' He also said that Loki the dog has more followers on Twitter than he does and is 'unquestionably better-looking, certainly better bred and a lot better known.'

When Liam and Danielle split for the first time in September 2012 Liam was very worried about Danielle and talked to *Now Magazine* about his concerns. He said: 'I'm not so much worried about me – whatever happens, I'll live and deal with it. I'm more concerned about Danielle because I don't want people harassing her for any reason.

'Obviously she's got a lot on her mind without people saying things on the internet or going to her doorstep.

'She doesn't need that right now. I've asked for people to stay away from her as much as possible so she can deal with things.'

When Liam and Danielle split the press suggested that Liam was dating former *X Factor* winner Leona Lewis, someone he had previously admitted was his 'celebrity crush'. In October 2012, Liam had told Radio 1: 'I do have a crush on Leona, she's hot. I have met her. She's hot. I haven't eaten dinner with her, though. I'd like to highlight the fact I'm single. I am single!'

Leona set the record straight in an interview with the *Mirror*, saying: 'Liam is a really sweet, lovely guy. I'm a fan of One Direction. We have been friends for a year-and-a-half.

'I know you have to ask [if we're dating]. I've learned from having relationships before that have been speculated about, it's best not to talk about it. I think that's important.

'Usually the other person doesn't get a say, so it's really one-sided and unfair.'

In a separate interview with *Look Magazine* she said: 'Liam is really sweet and lovely – very talented, and he is writing songs now as well. I feel like he is the one that keeps it all together for 1D. He is grounded, he comes from a stable home and he is very aware of what is going on in the music industry outside what he is doing, which I like.

'We talk a lot because we have a lot in common. We are friends.'

DID YOU KNOW?

If Liam had a son or daughter he would give them the name Taylor. He revealed to KRB Radio: 'I like the name Taylor. Taylor's pretty neutral for a boy or a girl – that's what I'm going to call my first child if I had children.'

Liam might be really good-looking and one of the biggest stars on the planet but he still gets tongue-tied when he sees a gorgeous girl, especially if she is famous. He was lost for words when he met *Transformers* actress and model Rosie Huntington-Whiteley at a photo shoot for *Glamour* magazine, admitting: 'I'm not the best at talking to women. When you're with someone like Rosie, it's a bit more difficult. I was like, I don't really know what to say, so I'm just gonna kind of stand here and try to be cool.'

Rosie described the boys as being 'like puppies – they're adorable. They've all got this sparkle in their eye and they're all just gorgeous. White, white eyes; shiny, shiny teeth.' They gave her free tickets to one of their concerts so she could come along and see them in action with her boyfriend, actor Jason Statham.

DID YOU KNOW?

If the boys were stuck in a lift with somebody, Liam thinks it would be best to be with someone funny, like comedian Michael McIntyre. The other boys would rather be stuck with somebody good-looking. Liam actually has Michael McIntyre's phone number in his phone and says after Harry, he is the most famous person in his phone book. The most famous person in Niall's phone book is Beyoncé!

CHAPTER NINE

FAMILY & FRIENDS

Liam's first year as a member of 1D was so busy that he hardly had any time off to see his family. His dad Geoff told the *Express & Star* in September 2011: 'We have only seen him about 30 days in the past year because he has been so busy. But that's just one of those things you have to face up to.'

When the boys embarked on their 'Up All Night' tour Liam's family and friends all went to see their Wolverhampton concert and Liam's family were so proud of him. There were about 30 of them in total, plus the families of the four other boys. Liam's family also attended the homecoming concerts for the other boys – they wanted to bond with Harry, Zayn, Niall and Louis' families. When the boys performed in Plymouth, Liam's proud grandad Ken went to see him as he lives in Cornwall, on the southwest coast of England. Before he went,

Liam's dad Geoff revealed to his local paper: 'He's 87 years old and he's never been to a pop concert in his life, but he's really looking forward to it.'

DID YOU KNOW?

1D don't want to be a boy band who dance a lot, they want to concentrate on singing. Zayn revealed to *Glamour* magazine: 'We didn't want to just follow the boy band formula. We didn't want to do any dancing, we just wanted to be five dudes in a band.' Liam added: 'We can't dance – we're a bit lazy. We're just normal lads, we look stupid dancing. That's what I think.'

Wolverhampton is over 130 miles from London but this doesn't stop Liam from visiting whenever he can, even if it is just for 48 hours. Rather than staying inside the house during his time there, his family go for meals out and do all the normal things they would do if Liam wasn't famous. His dad told the *Express & Star* about one visit. He said: 'We went for a carvery at the Cross Guns. A waiter commented on how much Liam looked like Liam Payne from One Direction. When he told him he was Liam, the guy brought about six members of female staff over. They all wanted to meet my son. It was great.'

Before he was famous Liam would go with his dad to his local pub quite often, even though he didn't drink. He really enjoys spending one-to-one time with Geoff. On 8 July 2012, Liam was visiting his family when he decided to do some cooking with his dad. He tweeted a photo of Geoff in the kitchen with the message 'Just cooking chinese with my dad and he's got his new gok wan cook book yumm!!!

'I'm excitedddd :D go on daddy payne'

In June 2013, Liam went to see *Ghost the Musical* at the

Grand Theatre in Wolverhampton with his family. During other visits they have gone for a meal out at the Penn Tandoori Indian restaurant, visited Strykers bowling alley in Bushbury, to the local cinema to watch a movie and to Pizza Hut. Liam might have eaten at really posh restaurants since joining 1D, but his favourite restaurant is the Cosmo Chinese in Wolverhampton. Staff in these places will often ask if he minds posing with them for a photo and he agrees willingly; he likes making people happy.

Liam made sure he got to his sister Nicole's fancy dress 21st birthday party – he wouldn't have missed it for the world. After deciding to go as his hero Batman, he looked online for the perfect costume. He saw an amazing one for £500 but when his mum found out, she told him it was far too expensive and he should go for something cheaper. Liam listened to her advice and bought one for £50 instead, and it still looked great. He really cares about what his family thinks and appreciates all the advice they give him. Although he knows that he should be careful with his money, he can't resist splurging out now and again.

When Liam is in London or travelling the world the family don't get too many fans turning up at their home but when a radio station decided to run a hidden treasure competition to win 1D concert tickets, lots of fans turned up in Wolverhampton and started searching through his family's garden. There were six cryptic clues, including 'could have been an ancient burial site' and 'they are close to somewhere beautiful'. Fans thought the answer was his family's home because that is where Liam grew up. Geoff didn't get angry but found the whole situation funny, ringing the radio station to explain what was happening.

Geoff told the *Sun*: 'I'm much better now that the

competition is over. I've had people loitering around the house for days on end now. I'm glad someone won it. There have been people hiding round corners, looking for them.'

When Liam found out that it was his former dance teacher's 30th birthday party in February 2013 he decided to make the trip up from Yorkshire, where he had been rehearsing with the other boys. Jodie Richards, who runs Pink Productions, was celebrating at the Britannia Hotel and was shocked when Liam walked in at 10pm. She explained to her local paper: 'I didn't know if he would be able to turn up so I didn't say anything to anyone. He text me on the Saturday morning to say he would be there, but I didn't think anything of it.

'Then at 7pm he text me to say he had finished rehearsals and had just left Wakefield. The first words he said to me when he arrived were, "Dee, I told you I wouldn't let you down."'

Liam couldn't make the trip on his own just in case he was ambushed by fans so he came with two bodyguards in a people carrier with blacked-out windows. When he first arrived, people didn't notice who he was but once a few of the girls recognised him, they started screaming. They couldn't believe their dance teacher knew Liam! Liam's family were also at the party because Jodie has become a good family friend over the years.

Liam is just Liam when he is at home and his family don't treat him any differently. For Christmas 2012, he got the *Toy Story* box set, chocolates, clothes, a model aeroplane and some Batman things. He was chuffed with all his presents because they were just what he wanted. He didn't get Harry, Zayn, Louis or Niall any presents and they didn't get him any either, as he explained to *Parade* magazine: 'I don't think we've ever bought each other a Christmas present. If it's somebody's birthday, I have to arrange the present – always late because I'm a bit lazy.'

He joked: 'I'm not about to become the Christmas Man as well. That's too many jobs!'

DID YOU KNOW?

Liam thinks the first *Toy Story* movie is the best because it's the original. He also loves the Adam Sandler movie, *Click*.

Because One Direction are so successful Liam is now a millionaire but he doesn't waste his money and instead chooses to treat his family to nice things. When journalists try to talk to him about money, he says he gets paid in sweets and is just enjoying the sweetshop. He doesn't feel the need to discuss money with strangers, and will only say that 1D have an accountant who looks after everything financial for them. When he went home for Christmas just a few weeks after *The X Factor* finished, he decided to treat his family to expensive gifts that he wouldn't have been able to afford before joining 1D. He bought them jewellery, iPads and a laptop – gifts to thank them for the support they had given him. His family were very touched, but just having him home for Christmas was the best present they could have asked for.

He bought his mum and dad a BMW car and treats his whole family to holidays in Florida when they need a break. When they visited Walt Disney World in September 2012, he had a blast, posing for photos with Mickey Mouse and tweeting, 'Had a great holiday so far! Disney was amazinggggg!' and 'Tower of Terror was amazing!' He enjoys spending time with his family and he is so thankful for every sacrifice they made when he was growing up and starting out on his journey to becoming a singer.

DID YOU KNOW?

For Liam's mum Karen the other boys are like the sons she never had – she considers them all members of the Payne family. When she sees 1D CDs in stores or sees fans walking around with Liam's face on their T-shirts, she feels really proud. It all seems like one long dream for her. When Liam and the other boys were asked by *Daybreak* how their mums deal with their fame, Liam replied: 'My mum just cries the whole time. My mum literally has not stopped crying for the past two-and-a-half years.'

DID YOU KNOW?

Liam's mum Karen still likes doing his washing for him! She misses him so much when he is away, especially on special days like his birthday.

As well as Liam being very close to his family, he is also close to Andy Samuels, his best friend before he became famous. If you want to follow Andy on Twitter, his address is: https://twitter.com/AndySamuels31. He has over 660,000 followers. His bio reads: 'Wassup. Im Andy. I make t-shirts and stuff. Everyday is a weekend. Ya feel.' Andy's T-shirt company is called My Box Clothing and he is also a dancer.

In an interview Andy did for LDN fashion he was asked when and where he looked his best. He replied: 'Not long ago, it was my best friend's birthday [Liam's 19th] and I don't know about looking my best, but I remember feeling good about how I looked and how I carried myself positively, so probably then. Until I got sprayed with champagne later that night – I didn't look great then.'

Liam and Andy do some great Twitcams for fans. When they were in France they did a great one at 5am about their experiences while clubbing and Liam joked that he wanted to swap Andy for a new friend because he was eating Pringles in his bed and getting crumbs everywhere! A girl came up to chat to them in the club but she thought they were too young. She ended up coming back and gave Andy her number. They didn't talk to many people because Liam was quite nervous – he finds it really hard talking to new people.

During the Twitcam, Liam said: 'I'm so tired today. It's mad like, these last few days, it's been crazy, doing a country every single day. It's so tiring. You literally land in a different country and it's the weirdest like, thing ever, like literally when we were in Sweden today, after I said "Hi Sweden" on *X Factor*, I was thinking, "Did I just say Hi Italy and I'm not in Italy or did I say Hi Sweden and I'm in Jamaica?" It's weird.'

If you haven't seen Liam's Twitcams then you should check them out on YouTube. He is really honest in them and answers as many fans' questions as he possibly can. You will see what Liam is like when not being interviewed by the press and he always does things to make fans laugh. Next time he does a live Twitcam, you should take part if you can – he reads out messages fans have sent him and you might even get a mention!

DID YOU KNOW?

If Liam was marooned on a desert island the three people he would like with him would be Andy, Ben Winston (Producer of *This Is Us*) and former *X Factor* judge Tulisa Contostavlos (so they could compare arm tattoos).

Most of Liam's other friends from Wolverhampton are at uni now so he has to remember to ring them when it is after

2pm UK time because otherwise they might be asleep. Liam thinks being in 1D is a bit like being a student – they get to have loads of fun, play on Fifa and watch the same kind of TV shows that students watch. He thinks they work a lot, lot, lot harder than students though and they have to watch TV on catch-up or on DVDs because most nights they are usually performing.

When Liam goes for a meal or a night out with close friends he had before he was famous he sometimes thinks he should pay the bill, but his friends don't expect him to. They don't want Liam to feel at all obliged and are happy to pay their share. Other people, like friends from school who he's not that close to, kind of expect him to buy them a drink if they bump into him on a night out.

One of Liam's famous friends is Great Britain diver Tom Daley. They became friends when Liam phoned Tom up after he was bombarded with nasty tweets during the 2012 Olympics. Tom received horrible abuse when he finished in fourth place in the 10m men's synchronised platform event because he didn't win a medal. Two people were even arrested for the tweets they sent – they were so abusive. Just a few days later, Tom went on to win a bronze medal in the 10m men's platform event.

Tom told the *Daily Star*: 'I'm really good mates with Liam – we actually became mates after the Twitter thing when that guy gave me abuse.

'Since then we've become close mates and usually on a typical boys' night, you'll find him and me down at Funky Buddha, having a few drinks and a dance.

'Either that or we'll go for a Chinese or a Wagamama.'

DID YOU KNOW?

For Halloween 2012 Liam dressed up as Batman and went to the Funky Buddha nightclub with Tom and Andy. Tom was wearing an inflatable skeleton costume and Andy was dressed as a zombie!

The member of the group that Liam is most protective of is Niall and he would do anything to help him if he was in a bad situation. All of the boys feel like they should look after him, even though Harry is the youngest. Liam also feels for Zayn because he has had a terrible time on Twitter, receiving lots of racist tweets.

Above: During their time on the *X Factor*, One Direction had the opportunity to visit the iconic Abbey Road zebra crossing. They took a bit of a different photo from The Beatles though!

Below Left: Where it all began… Liam looking relaxed outside the *X Factor* studios.

Below Right: The Daredevil: Liam pulls a funny face in New Zealand while bungee jumping.

Above: The boys chill-out backstage while on tour in America.

Below: Appearing at the *Men in Black 3* premiere, the band look dangerous with their Nerf guns in hand.

Above Left: Liam and his friend, Olympic diver Tom Daley, go out in fancy dress for Halloween.

Above Right: Liam looked focussed when he arrived for the 2013 MTV Video Music Awards.

Below: One Direction had their first taste of the movie business and were excited on the red carpet for their film *One Direction: All About Us*.

Liam looked very
dashing in a sharp suit at
the American Music
Awards in 2013.

CHAPTER TEN

FAN LOVE

1D's fans mean the world to Liam and the rest of the boys and they are so grateful for the support they receive. In July 2012, he was asked by Tumblr's Storyboard about their devoted fans. He said: 'It's very flattering, obviously, as we can see how much they care for us. We just hope they're crying tears of joy! None of us could obviously ever have imagined this just two years ago. I don't think anyone could have seen this coming, to be honest.'

He was also asked: 'Is it ever stressful, knowing that there are literally millions of people analysing your every move?' to which he replied: 'I wouldn't say it's stressful at all. Since *The X Factor* our lives have obviously changed, but I would say for the better. We have millions of fans that support us and we get to meet them while travelling all over the world.'

On 2 August 2012, Liam and Niall decided to surprise fans shopping at the Westfield London Shopping Centre in Shepherds Bush with an acoustic performance. They just appeared, walked over to where there was a little stage by the escalators and started singing, with Niall playing his guitar. Fans couldn't believe their eyes and ears; they were astonished that they were seeing Liam and Niall perform 'What Makes You Beautiful'. After they had finished, they simply got up and left, with fans following them.

The boys like receiving cards and gifts from fans but they really love the scrapbooks fans have made and the drawings they have done. They appreciate the time it has taken to create something in their likeness or to put together a scrapbook. And they love how they can mention wanting a particular cereal or chocolate bar on Twitter and the next day a fan will turn up at their hotel with the exact same item they mentioned. They do get strange gifts sometimes, though. Liam was once given a Stanley knife and Louis received a live hermit crab! The best present Zayn ever received was a birthday cake from a four-year-old for his nineteenth birthday. He was chilling at home with his family when he heard a knock at the door and when he opened it, she was standing there, holding it. One of Liam's favourite gifts was a teddy bear that a fan had made of his girlfriend at the time. He really loves getting superhero action figures from fans – he doesn't mind what superhero either because he loves them all.

The weirdest question a fan has ever asked Liam was whether she could lick his face. This really freaked him out – he couldn't understand why anyone would want to lick someone else's face. When the boys visited Niagara Falls on a day off in May 2012 they were driven in two police cars to a nearby arcade. A fan tried to break into one of the cars and got arrested. Liam found it all very extreme. He also finds it weird when fans try to hide in garbage bins or pretend to work in hotels just to get close to him and the other boys. A fan once managed to get into the changing rooms at a gym when he was getting changed, which is a little freaky. Liam deserves to be able to get changed without being hassled.

DID YOU KNOW?

Niall, Harry, Louis and Zayn like to call Liam the 'Gary Barlow' of 1D. Liam doesn't mind, though, because Take That's Gary Barlow is someone he looks up to. Niall told the *Sun*: 'Liam has that Barlow aura. He says things like, "Come on, boys, let's roll; let's get going." He knows it and can't deny it.'

Although Liam might seem happy all the time to fans, in October 2012 he was finding things too much and went to see a doctor, who told him that his stress levels were dangerously high. He revealed to *Now Magazine*: 'I was ill. I was told I was stressed, so I had to get everything checked out. I didn't think I was, but someone told me I was. As a result, I went to get a blood test. I'd never had one before, so I held my breath when I was getting it done. That caused me to go into a fit.'

Thankfully, he was fine and after taking time to rest, he began to feel much better. He added: 'I think sometimes I don't realise how much the pressure gets to me but as long as we've got each other to support each other, we'll be fine, I suppose.'

If Liam had to compare American fans to British fans he would say that US fans try to get noticed more and that they are more tanned. He can remember seeing a young fan when 1D were supporting Big Time Rush in 2012, who really stood out from the crowd because he was wearing a huge hat that he had made himself using lots of Sellotape, Crayola marker pens and a potato. Liam also spotted a girl with a lampshade on her head. Harry thinks the biggest difference between British and American fans is that British fans wear a lot more coats. Zayn thinks the main difference is their accents and that American girls are a bit more confident.

If you ever go to a 1D CD or book signing, make sure you take some Silly String with you. Liam loves it when fans bring some along with them because it wakes everyone up and they can have a minute or two of fun and rest their signing hands at the same time.

DID YOU KNOW?

When Liam and Harry were coming down with colds in America, they had to have an injection in their bums to try to boost their immune systems.

Liam and the rest of the boys were thrilled to have the opportunity to do a 3D concert movie for fans. *This Is Us* was released on 29 August 2013 in the UK, and 30 August in America. Before it came out, Liam told MTV: 'It's going to be amazing for us to look on in, like, however many years and just be, like, "This is when I was a lad".'

Louis added: 'You know what we always say, when we left home to do *X Factor* our parents were like, "Make sure you take loads of pictures", but we've got a film to do that for us now so we can be lazy.'

The One Direction movie was directed by *Super Size Me* director Morgan Spurlock. Niall explained how it was filmed at a press conference. He said: 'Cameras have been with us every day for the last few months and it's been great. We were lucky that when we started we had a background on *The X Factor* and were somewhat used to it.

'So we didn't really feel like it was that intrusive and don't mind the cameras — we just want to get involved as much as we can. It's going to be a really good movie. The fans know us, but they don't really get to see what goes on behind the scenes and the movie will allow for that, show the other bits, what we're like off stage.

'There's only so much personality in terms of the connection between us as a five that you can get from Twitter or anything like short interviews.'

DID YOU KNOW?

When the boys perform they sometimes challenge each other to throw in random words or during interviews, give the most random answers just for fun.

CHAPTER ELEVEN

LOOKING GOOD

Harry might be the member of 1D with the most famous hair but Liam's hairstyles are also popular with fans. In fact his hairstyle has changed more than any other member of One Direction. Before he appeared on *The X Factor* he went to the same hairdressers as his mum and sister, Royston Blythe Hair Saloon in Wolverhampton. His favourite hairdresser was called Ashley Gamble. Liam helped the salon raise money at a charity event they put on by singing for free.

The owner of the hair salon, Royston, told the *Birmingham Mail*: 'He's a very professional person, he's a very well-mannered young man and that's an added bonus because he's a great singer as well. Even from the age of fifteen he had a great voice. When he came to the shop, he was such a nice lad and when we first heard him sing, we just knew he'd got it. We just knew he was going to get bigger and bigger.

'He was always a pin-up, even before he went on the show. All our juniors like him.'

When the boys made *The X Factor* live shows they were each given a makeover by the *X Factor* hairdressers and styling team but Liam's new look was awful! Poor Liam was given 'Lego helmet hair' and received lots of flak for it in the press and from fans. Thankfully, he managed to get them to change it so it looked a lot more like his original style and posted a photo on Twitter with the message, 'Hair been redone much happier.'

When Liam grew his hair and had it curly he really liked it, but he got sick of people saying he had hair like Harry. His hair is naturally curly but he had spent six years straightening it, so people wrongly thought his hair was naturally straight. In the end he had it cut shorter to look more like *Twilight* actor Taylor Lautner's hair.

DID YOU KNOW?

Liam has admitted if a movie were to be made about 1D he would like Taylor Lautner to play him. Harry would choose Orlando Bloom and Louis thinks Leonardo DiCaprio would be the perfect actor to play him.

In September 2012, Liam boldly decided to shave his hair off, even though this wasn't allowed. He confessed to *Vogue* magazine: 'At the start, management said I wasn't allowed to change my hair but then I did it anyway, so they kind of let that one go.

'I tend to change my hair quite a lot. I can go out and about. The other day I went out dressed as a big chav – Adidas trainers, jogging bottoms – and no one recognised me.'

In another interview with BBC Radio 1, he explained how he did it. He said: 'I was doing a photo shoot for a certain magazine, and they said, "What can we do with your hair?", and I was like, shave it off!

'We went shorter, and shorter, and this is it. I have naturally quite curly hair, so I had to straighten it every morning with a hairdryer. My mum was worried about me – she thought I'd got some clippers and done it myself.'

DID YOU KNOW?

Liam's favourite colour is purple and he once confessed to having a set of pink hair straighteners.

Fashionwise Liam likes to keep it simple, wearing T-shirts with cardigans and blazers. He often wears T-shirts that his friend Andy has designed. His big weakness is buying lots of trainers and high-tops, although his favourites are white Converse. He has size eight feet, just like Niall and Zayn. The other boys think Liam has the worst fashion style, as Louis explained to *Top of the Pops* magazine: 'Liam once sat in the car and it took us 20 minutes before we looked down and noticed that he was wearing leopard-print shoes. We were baffled!'

Louis might not rate Liam's style but as their stylist, Caroline Watson, commented to *Look Magazine*: 'Liam's got the most expensive taste. He'll say, "Oh, I've seen this Dior jacket I like," and I think, "Uh oh".'

Caroline also revealed that Harry will sneak off with some of the outfits he has borrowed, saying: 'Harry's terrible for taking clothes. We'll do a shoot and some jeans will be missing, then I'll see a picture of them on a night out.'

Since joining the group Liam has got a few tattoos, even though his mum isn't a big tattoo fan. He has a quote on his arm that reads: 'Everything I ever wanted, but nothing that I'll ever need'. He explained to British radio DJ Scott Mills during an album Ustream what it means. He said: 'It's basically that obviously we've got a lot of things from doing this and stuff, and there are things that I want, but all I ever need is my family and these four boys right here.'

He also has 'Only time will tell' on his left wrist and a four-arrow tattoo on his right forearm. When fans saw the arrow tattoo, they thought the arrows represented the other boys, all pointing in one direction. He also has a feather tattoo on his right arm and a screw on his ankle. Liam got his screw tattoo at the same time as Louis got one, to match the screw tattoos Zayn and Harry already had. Louis tweeted: 'So me and Liam joined the crew yesterday and got two screw tattoos on our ankles, now we all have it except Niall! Come on @NiallOfficial.' Niall tweeted back that he would get it done.

Liam's sister Ruth hadn't known that Liam was getting a tattoo, so she tweeted her followers to ask them what design he had chosen. Louis' girlfriend Eleanor tweeted her back, saying: '@RuthPayne0990 Don't worry they're tiny! Like tiny little plus signs xx'.

Liam isn't vain, but he likes to look good so will often work out when he's got a spare hour or two. He finds exercising helps relieve any stress he might be feeling and gives him time to think. He has loved exercising ever since he used to go for all those runs before school.

CHAPTER TWELVE

TOURING

Liam loves touring, especially when he gets to visit places he has never seen before. He gets a real buzz when they are performing in a new country and the fans start singing their songs back at them. Liam and the boys like to set the fans challenges for when they see them in concert. In May 2013, Liam tweeted Norwegian fans to say: 'Hi everyone for tomorrow's gig everyone has to wear ski goggles in kiss you so make sure to bring them with youuuuuu #NorwaySkiDay1D' and tweeted Dutch fans to say: 'Hi everyone if your coming to the Amsterdam gig tomorrow you have to wear orange!!!! Have tooooo!! :)! Thanks #turnziggoorange'.

When they are on the road, the two things he can't live without are his laptop and his phone – he needs them so he can contact his family and friends back home. Before he goes on stage he has to hand over his mobile to a member of the crew to look after it, but he feels apprehensive about it because if they lost it, he would have no one to talk to until he got another phone.

The boys try to make every show lots of fun for the fans and different from the previous one. Liam explained to 3 News what fans can expect when they come to see one of their concerts. He said: 'On our show we like to get the audience involved as much as possible. We read out a few twitters and stuff on stage that people have sent in so they might expect to see their twitter on stage or something. That'll be quite exciting and just us having a good time on stage, you know, [we hope] they have as much fun as we do.'

Liam especially loved taking their 'Up All Night' Tour to Australia and New Zealand in April 2012. He, Zayn, Harry, Niall and Louis had only been in Australia for a matter of hours when they went sunbathing on a luxury yacht in Sydney Harbour. They had great fun swimming and splashing around in the water. A few days later they visited a koala sanctuary and Liam learnt how to surf with Louis, something he will never forget.

Liam told Olly Murs on *The Xtra Factor*: 'It's strange, with some countries that we haven't even been to, people know, like, everything about you. That's like the strangest thing for me. I think when we went surfing [points at Louis] in Australia, and we were in the sea and we got recognised, and there was that helicopter was flying over us.' (The helicopter was from the Channel 9 News team.)

Because the boys live with each other 24/7 when touring, they really know each other inside out and know each other's bad habits. The boys say Niall's worst crime is farting, Louis' antisocial quality is having smelly feet, Liam's annoying behaviour is going to the gym all the time, Zayn's is having the window down in the bus, even when it's cold, and Harry has two bad habits – snoring with his mouth open and taking food from their plates. The other boys also hate the fact that Liam says 'brilliant' and 'fantastic' all the time!

DID YOU KNOW?

Liam's favourite vegetable is asparagus. Harry prefers sweetcorn and Louis likes potatoes the best.

Sometimes the press like to suggest that Liam will one day go solo and tour on his own but he insists this won't happen. In an interview with the *Sun* he said: 'I think it would be massively, massively boring. I don't know how Justin Bieber does it, but full props to him.

'I like being around the boys, I enjoy other people's company and it's a lot more fun being in a band on stage.'

DID YOU KNOW?

While the boys were in Australia and New Zealand in 2012, Danielle Peazer was looking after Liam's two pet turtles, Boris and Archimedes, at home. He told the hosts of Australian talk show, *The Project*, that he had had to split them up because one turtle had bitten off the other turtle's foot!

Liam loves being adventurous and went bungee jumping with Louis when they had a day off in New Zealand. They jumped at night from the legendary Sky Tower – which is 328 metres (1,076 ft) tall. Liam loved the thrill of the jump and the fact that he bungee jumped in the place where the sport was invented. The boys were supported by Harry and their hairstylist, Lou Teasdale, and her baby, Lux. If you search on YouTube, you can see a short video that a fan managed to take and a video that Liam and Louis filmed of themselves right at the top and as they jumped. Liam managed to talk to the camera all the way down and said it was so incredible, he would recommend anyone visiting New Zealand should do it. Zayn wouldn't do it in a million years though, because he is really scared of heights.

DID YOU KNOW?

When they visited Japan in 2013 Liam admitted that if he could choose to be any animal, he would pick a giraffe so he would be really tall.

When they went to Norway in May 2013 Liam took his friend Andy Samuels with him and they went on a speedboat ride together. It was very sunny and they took a video, which you can check out on YouTube. They are both wearing shades and Liam hasn't got a top on. Andy says: 'So we are in Norway on a boat, chilling. You know how it is!'

When he posted the video online he wrote: 'Today was actually an amazing day, Norway is one of my favourite places ever!!! Me and @Real_Liam_Payne love it.'

The boys like to have fun while they are travelling and enjoy filming themselves doing weird dances to songs like Katy Perry's 'Firework' and Carly Rae Jepsen's 'Call Me Maybe'. While travelling on their tour bus, they play cards, watch movies, play on their PlayStation and chat about all kinds of things. They also like updating their Twitter accounts and Liam likes following as many fans as possible. Being on the road for many hours can get very tiring so when they arrive at their hotel for the night they just want to sleep. Sometimes Zayn forgets this and at 1 o'clock in the morning, Liam has to bang on his door to tell him to turn his music down. Even when they eventually get to sleep, often they are woken at 5 or 6am by fans singing their songs outside. Even if they are 10 floors up, they can still hear them because Directioners sing loud. Liam and the rest of the boys find it flattering, but they're not sure what the other hotel guests think!

Liam loves touring America and Canada and felt privileged to support Big Time Rush in February 2012. When they performed in Toronto at The Air Canada Centre he wore a Raptors basketball vest, as did Louis. Niall, Zayn and Harry wore blue-and-white Toronto Maple Leafs ice-hockey tops. Just before their performance, the boys managed to lock their tour manager, Paul Higgins, in a toilet. The next day Liam wrote on Facebook: 'I had the most amazing time last night. You guys were LOUD we could hear every word! Hopefully we can come back and do our own shows soon. Lots of Love Liam x.' He also tweeted: 'Toronto was amazing last night cant wait to do it all again :)'

DID YOU KNOW?

Liam once forgot his words three times during one show. It was the second show they ever did, so to cover himself he pretended that his microphone wasn't working. On another occasion Harry accidentally sang the words to a later verse, which messed things up a bit!

Liam has always loved America because he thinks American people are very welcoming and friendly, and he loves the hot weather. When they are in America, Liam and Louis often spend their days off together, doing touristy things. In September 2012, they went swimming with sharks at Miami Seaquarium when they visited Florida. While in California, Liam and a few of the others went fishing and Liam caught a baby shark! He told the *Sun*: 'We went fishing in San Diego. It was only my second time ever fishing and we had such great fun.

'We went fishing for half an hour and there was nothing at all. Then I pulled out a baby tiger shark.'

After they had stroked it, he released it back into the ocean. Sandy Beales, base guitarist in the boys' band, tweeted: 'Ridiculous night out on a boat in San Diego, @Real_Liam_Payne even caught a shark, yeah a shark, It's my main phobia but I gave it a stroke.'

Josh Devine, their drummer, tweeted: 'Had a late night fishing trip... @Real_Liam_Payne caught a baby tiger shark. felt very weird to touch such a killer.'

On another day off during their time in America, Liam went exploring in New York with Niall. He ended up getting his shirt ripped and hit in the face after being ambushed by fans. Liam explained what happened to YouTube star Andrea Russett. He said: 'We were in New York and we left the hotel. Usually when you leave the hotel, you say "hi" to everybody, then you just stroll up the street about your own business – it's usually fine. But this time, as we went up the street, we got about six blocks up and I realised there were still, like, 600 people following us behind and then our security guard bent down to tie his shoe and they just went… we were surrounded by people. It was so crazy; that has been the most crazy experience so far for me. It was mad!'

Liam tweeted later: 'Guys i do really appriciate your support and love you all but sometimes it all gets too crazy for me.'

DID YOU KNOW?

Liam has a phobia of spoons. He told *OK! Magazine*: 'In restaurants, when I don't know where the spoons have been, I can't use them but I can use all the other cutlery.' He also refuses to share a drink with other people because hygiene matters a lot to him.

During their tour dates in America the boys are allowed to request whatever food and drink they like for their dressing rooms, so Liam asks for Yorkshire tea and Niall requests Irish sausages. Both items are hard to get hold of in America. (Liam can't see why Niall loves Irish sausages so much because when he tried them, he couldn't taste any difference between them and normal sausages.) The venues normally provide lots of water, energy drinks, fruit and sweets as standard, so the boys always have something to munch on before they go onstage.

On 16 May 2013, the boys unveiled the details of their 2014 stadium tour, 'Where We Are', at Wembley Stadium. They would be touring the UK, Ireland and South America. During the press conference they were asked by MTV where they see themselves in ten years' time. Liam answered: 'We want to do this for as long as we can, really.

'We came to watch Take That at Wembley when they were doing their stadium tour and we couldn't believe how big it was, so if we can emulate something like that, I think that's the way to go.'

Louis added: 'For us, it's more about keeping our feet on the ground and taking every day as it comes. That would be great, but at the moment we are just set for the stadiums – I can't believe I'm saying it!'

DID YOU KNOW?

Liam would like 1D to sing a song in Spanish one day. Louis would struggle because he is hopeless at languages, but Niall is great at speaking Spanish and French so he would do really well.

As well as loving touring around the world, the boys enjoy the concerts they do in the UK and Ireland; they just love coming home and thanking the fans who have been with them since the beginning. In an interview with Gordon Smart from the *Sun*, Louis admitted: 'Niall turned up recently at a gig with a Segway. We were all spinning about on it, then Harry decided to strip off and go streaking. He turned a few heads.'

Niall thought he was brave because as the temperature drops, the faster you go. Liam also confessed: 'I pulled Harry's trousers down on stage one night. What I hadn't considered was that I might whip his pants off by accident too – which happened!'

That night the show was being recorded for the 3D movie but the incident wasn't included in the final cut, for obvious reasons!

The boys also stripped off when they visited Aberdeen. Even though it was really cold, they decided to go skinny-dipping. They took some photos but they are well hidden away so that no one from the press can get hold of them. Liam found it funny that Harry stripped completely naked, but refused to take his shoes off!

Here are the boys' set lists:

TOURING

'UP ALL NIGHT' TOUR SET LIST

1. 'Na Na Na'
2. 'Stand Up'
3. 'I Wish'
4. Medley of 'I Gotta Feeling'/'Stereo Hearts'/'Valerie'/'Torn'
5. 'Moments'
6. 'Gotta Be You'
7. 'More Than This'
8. 'Up All Night'
9. 'Tell Me A Lie'
10. 'Everything About You'
11. 'Use Somebody'
12. 'One Thing'
13. 'Save You Tonight'
14. 'What Makes You Beautiful'
    Encore:
15. 'I Want'

'TAKE ME HOME' TOUR SET LIST

1. 'Up All Night'
2. 'I Would'
3. 'Heart Attack'
4. 'More Than This'
5. 'Loved You First'
6. 'One Thing'
7. 'C'mon, C'mon'
8. 'Change My Mind'
9. 'One Way Or Another (Teenage Kicks)'
10. 'Last First Kiss'
11. 'Moments'
12. 'Back For You'

13. 'Summer Love'
14. 'Over Again'
15. 'Little Things'
16. 'Teenage Dirtbag' (Wheatus cover)
17. 'Rock Me'
18. 'She's Not Afraid'
19. 'Kiss You'
20. 'Live While We're Young'
21. 'What Makes You Beautiful'

CHAPTER THIRTEEN

SPECIAL MOMENTS

Being in One Direction has given Liam so many opportunities that he wouldn't have had otherwise. In November 2012, he managed to meet Jay-Z while the boys were in America. Liam tweeted afterwards to tell fans, saying: 'Alssoooo my biggest news todayy I met one of my idols and couldn't even look him in the eye.'

Liam likes listening to Jay-Z and Kanye West's music, which most people think is unusual because they're not in the same musical genre as 1D. He also likes listening to Ed Sheeran's albums and considers the 'Lego House' singer a friend. He really enjoyed recording Ed's track 'Moments' for the *Up All Night Yearbook* edition, and working with Ed on 'Little Things' and 'Over Again' for *Take Me Home*. Liam also listens to music by artists and bands that aren't mainstream and really rates a singer called 'Passenger' (Mike Rosenberg) and his single 'Let Her Go'.

Liam loved having the opportunity to meet Will Smith, telling Drex & Maney from the Kiss 95.1FM Breakfast Show: 'Will Smith was the most exciting [celebrity we have met]. But the one we're most excited about going to meet is... well, me and Louis recently took up surfing and have been surfing quite a lot... and we actually might be going surfing with Kelly Slater, who's the best surfer in the world!'

Another special moment for Liam was having the opportunity to act in the hit Nickelodeon show *iCarly*, starring Miranda Cosgrove. Although he wasn't playing a character, just himself, the cameo still required Liam to use his acting abilities. When it aired on TV for the first time on 7 April 2012, the episode was seen by 3.9 million people. The boys also appeared on the American hit comedy sketch show *Saturday Night Live* that month as the episode's musical guests. This appearance was even more daunting as 37 million plus tune in each week and even some big actors and actresses have failed to make the right impression on the show as they have not been able to make the audience laugh. The host for the night was actress Sofia Vergara, who plays Gloria in *Modern Family*. The boys performed 'One Thing' and 'What Makes You Beautiful' and took part in a sketch where they had to wear wigs and moustaches. Check it out on YouTube if you haven't already seen it – it's really funny!

One of Liam's favourite performances of 2012 was performing at Madison Square Garden, New York City because everything went perfectly. His family had made the trip over to America and he liked popping up out of the stage floor during the show. While in New York, Liam's family checked out the temporary 1D store but the cops had to be called when they were recognised by fans (Liam wasn't even with them). Liam likes to joke that his parents are more famous than he is! During the visit, they all went to the Empire State Building together, with security guards there to protect them just in case things got out of control. Liam's dad Geoff sometimes forgets that his son is hugely famous and thinks that they can just walk around like normal people.

Liam was also very excited when 1D were invited to perform 'One Thing' at the 2012 MTV Video Music Awards (VMAs) for the first time. He told MTV before they performed: 'It's quite nerve-wracking, because obviously there's been so many historical moments and stuff that have happened at the VMAs.

'Now we want to make a moment ourselves, but who knows?

'I think performing at the VMAs is such a huge occasion... I think it ranks up there with one of the best performances we'll do so far.'

Not only did the boys get to perform but they also picked up three awards: Best Artist, Most Share-Worthy Video and Best Pop Video for 'What Makes You Beautiful'.

DID YOU KNOW?

1D's former bodyguard Andy Davies ('Baldy' to the boys) might not work for them anymore but he can't help but praise them for being 'polite, kind-hearted and very well-mannered'. He told the *Sunday Mirror* that Liam is the most 'businesslike' and 'sensible' of all the boys. Andy used to have to roam outside the boys' hotel rooms at night to stop fans from knocking on their doors and waking them up.

Liam has always enjoyed celebrating his birthday. When he turned eighteen, he asked fans not to send him presents but instead to give the money they would have spent to charity. He tweeted: 'For my birthday I would like everyone to visit cancerresearchuk.org and donate as much as they can to help fight cancer.'

For his nineteenth birthday Liam celebrated with his friends on 25 August, even though his birthday wasn't until 29 August. The party was organised by Danielle Peazer as they were dating at the time and it was held at the Funky Buddha club in London. Poor Niall nearly didn't get in because the bouncer outside didn't recognise him, but he eventually made it inside! Liam was presented with a huge Batman cake, which he loved and he made sure he posted up a picture on Twitter so the fans didn't miss out.

He tweeted: 'Can't believe today Danielle arranged me a surprise party had all my friends down what a great day.'

Danielle loved the party too, tweeting: 'What a day!!! So grateful to everyone that helped make Liam's surprise party possible.

'A few obstacles, but Sunday was such a perfect day in the end.

'It was very stressful but so worth it :) xx'

In the past, Liam has joked that his favourite song is 'Happy Birthday' because it means presents and if he could be any food, he would choose to be a birthday cake. It is funny that he loves birthdays so much because one of his big fears is getting older. He once tweeted fans to say: 'Guys i really want to follow everyone who sent me a bday card & thank you all but sometimes i just cant understand the writing :(sorry guys'.

A huge highlight for Liam was performing in the London 2012 Olympic Games Closing Ceremony, with four billion people watching. The boys sang 'What Makes You Beautiful' on top of a lorry as it circled the inside of the stadium. His family were so proud. Liam had always dreamt of competing at the Olympics when he was running but he wouldn't swap being in 1D for anything. He loves singing too much!

DID YOU KNOW?

That night he chatted to the Spice Girls, who had also performed in the Closing Ceremony, and he got to kiss Mel B, Mel C, Geri and Emma on the cheek!

LIAM'S TOP OLYMPIC TWEETS:

'100m im soo excited sooo buzzing im nervous i never get nervous whats goin onn!!!!'

'Team GB are doing amazinnggg in the olympics!'

'Olympic ceremony was amazziinnggg! So greatfull that they asked us to perform! A performance that ill never ever forget !!! :)'

Another special day for Liam was running around with the Real Madrid football team on 23 May 2013 at their training ground. He couldn't believe that they would get to meet huge stars such as Cristiano Ronaldo and Sergio Ramos – but the footballers were equally starstruck to meet Liam, Niall and Louis. They posted photos of themselves meeting the boys on Twitter, with Cristiano tweeting: 'Nice to meet @onedirection today.'

Niall summed up how the 1D boys felt when he tweeted: 'Up there with some of the best days of my life! Training with Real Madrid !dreams are made of that stuff.

'Massive thank you on behalf of me and the lads to Real Madrid, Jose mourinho, all the players! Unbelievable experience.

'All the players were really nice to us! And the gaffer I like to call him mr. Mourinho! still can't believe it!'

When Liam's friend Tom from back home heard that Liam had been training with Real Madrid, he was very jealous and jokingly tweeted: 'I hate @Real_Liam_Payne right now… Like im gonna kidnap him soon! Luckiest guy ever. Lmao.'

Some Directioners saw Tom's tweet and wrongly thought he was a hater so they sent him lots of abusive tweets. Tom decided to set the record straight so he tweeted: 'Okay serious tweet! I know @Real_Liam_Payne he's like my Lil bro! We were having banter! I don't hate him in the slightest! I love him! Lmao', but that still didn't stop the messages. In the end, Liam himself had to intervene, writing 'Hi everyone @tomqueens is actually one of my best friends please stop sending him threats aha thanks.'

Liam and Tom have been close friends for over ten years, so Liam naturally wanted to put things right. He values all of his friends, those he has been friends with for years and those he has only been friends with for a little while. He considers Directioners to be good friends and loves spending time with them online or in person.

CHAPTER FOURTEEN

TAKE ME
HOME

The boys' second album was *Take Me Home* and it was released on 9 November 2012. Liam was really pleased with how the album turned out, telling *Sunday Night*: 'I think the songs on this album are a bit more meaningful than the last album and I think that's the main difference, really. We wrote a lot of them and that's good news.

'I just think because of all the touring we've done, our voices have got that bit better.'

TAKE ME HOME TRACK LISTING:
1. 'Live While We're Young'
2. 'Kiss You'
3. 'Little Things'
4. 'C'mon, C'mon'

5. 'Last First Kiss'
6. 'Heart Attack'
7. 'Rock Me'
8. 'Change My Mind'
9. 'I Would'
10. 'Over Again'
11. 'Back for You'
12. 'They Don't Know About Us'
13. 'Summer Love'

Part of the reason why the boys chose the album title, *Take Me Home*, is because of how much they miss home when they are travelling. They love touring the world but they do get homesick after being away for long stretches at a time. For the album cover they had Liam lying on top of a red phone box, with his legs dangling down and Louis is sitting on Zayn's shoulder, reaching up to grab Liam's arm so he doesn't fall off. Niall is inside, making a call and Harry stands outside, with his arms crossed. It's a very iconic cover and fans loved it the second they saw it.

The songwriters and producers from the first album also worked on the second album, something the boys were pleased about because they got on so well and understood the kind of music the group wanted to make. Songwriter Savan Kotecha explained to Billboard why he thinks 1D have been successful in America, stating: 'It felt like everyone tried to do boy bands by going to the cool, hip producers who were coming up.

'We wanted to make it very vanilla. You're aiming for teens and tweens with boy band guilty pleasure music. We weren't trying to be urban or rhythmic, and they happened to share the same vision.'

The boys loved having the opportunity to write tracks

with some of the best songwriters and producers in the world. Liam explained to Billboard how the writing process worked. He said: 'It was actually usually groups of three. It's nice to have two people around. When you have more than two people working together it gets a bit unfocused as an idea. We tend to pair off a little bit. It was nice on this album because the room was laid out to write the songs. We'd work with a topline writer and just write about whatever we were thinking about that day.'

Liam also spoke about the recording process, adding: 'It was crazy – we only had a month or so to record the whole album, but we always felt like we had the fans on our side. They're always anxious to know where we are – even before I do! Like today, we've been staying at the Trump Hotel all week and they've been greeting us when we leave and when we come back. It's good to see that level of dedication.'

DID YOU KNOW?
Savan Kotecha thinks that Liam is developing into a great songwriter. Maybe one day he will write songs for artists other than One Direction.

Simon Cowell is thrilled that the boys have been so successful and have become global stars because he thinks they deserve it. He told *Heat Magazine*: 'We have the very best team imaginable for the boys.

'They are the most grounded artists I've ever worked with. They're really nice boys, so there are no tantrums. It's my job to make sure they are happy.'

Liam had been really looking forward to the album coming out because he couldn't wait to find out what fans thought of their new material. He admitted to the *Metro*: 'We've been feeling massive pressure. I think before we started recording songs we were quite pressured by it.

'But now we've recorded the tracks, we're all proud of what we've done. I love all the songs that are on the album so far, so it's been amazing and we just can't wait for people to hear them.

'When we make new songs you get them in your head, and then you start to try to sing it out loud when you're in the supermarket or out shopping somewhere.

'And then you think, "I can't sing that out loud because it's not out yet".'

The boys released three tracks from the album: 'Live While We're Young' on 28 September 2012, 'Little Things' on 12 November 2012 and 'Kiss You' on 8 February 2013. All three were hit singles around the world. 'Kiss You' was the first video that they had shot with director Vaughan Arnell, which was set in a studio rather than being outside on location. They wanted to get across their fun side and give the fans something tongue-in-cheek rather than being totally serious.

The boys released 'One Way or Another (Teenage Kicks)' on 17 February 2013. It wasn't a track from the album but a single for the charity Comic Relief. A cover of Blondie and The Undertones, it went to No. 1 in 63 countries.

The boys filmed the video for the single on tour and in Ghana at a school for children who live in a slum. For Liam, having the opportunity to see where the money they raised would be used was eye-opening. He played with the children from the school, saw babies getting vaccinations that would save them from dying of preventable diseases and saw how adults were being trained so they could get work and feed their families. Visiting a hospital emergency ward was very emotional for him. He knew that the money 'One Way Or Another

(Teenage Kicks)' raised would save thousands of lives and felt blessed that One Direction had been given the opportunity to record the single for such a good cause.

While in Ghana the boys were filmed so that clips of their trip could be shown on the *Comic Relief* TV programme. Liam told the cameras: 'It must be so difficult seeing your baby so ill. At home we take vaccinations for granted but not all children here have access to them and that can mean the difference between life and death.

'I've watched Red Nose Day appeals before and been in tears but seeing these babies so sick is another level of sadness. You just don't realise how hard life can be in other parts of the world.'

Zayn also pleaded with the viewers watching to do something, saying: 'It's so hard. I've never seen anything, never experienced anything like this in my life. The babies aren't even a year old.

'We all waste money but the most important thing we can all do is give £5 to protect children from these illnesses.'

The 2013 Red Nose Day/Comic Relief fundraiser raised a record £75 million – thanks in part to One Direction who raised over £2 million from sales of their single. Liam and the boys were so grateful to all the Directioners who bought 'One Way or Another (Teenage Kicks)' and would love to release another Red Nose Day single in the future.

MIDNIGHT MEMORIES

The boys' third album, *Midnight Memories*, was released on 25 November 2013. Before it was released, Louis told the press: 'There will be a new album this year with a rockier and edgier tone to it.'

Liam added: 'We've written a lot of the songs on it and we got the chance to work with a lot of great writers. It's a bit more edgy. It's grown as we've grown.'

The first single they released from the album was 'Best Song Ever'. Fans could preorder on iTunes from 26 June and the track was released on 22 July. However, the boys were disappointed when a rough copy of the song's audio was leaked a day early, with Niall telling Australian station Nova FM: 'Because it was leaked today, obviously it's a little bit frustrating 'cause we were wanting the fans to hear it.'

Of course Liam and the boys wanted the fans to hear the proper version, not something that was incomplete.

DID YOU KNOW?

At the start of the 'Best Song Ever' there is a sample of 'Baba O'Riley' by The Who.

In the video the boys all get dressed up as different characters. Harry is a marketing guy called Marcel, Niall is a studio executive (Harvey), Liam is a choreographer (Leroy), Louis is a studio executive (Johnny) and Zayn is a woman called Georgia Rose (the love interest in the video). It aired for the first time on 22 July 2013.

Harry loves the track and told Radio 1's Scott Mills: '"Best Song Ever" is my favourite song that we have done so far… it's kind of a little bit heavier. We're not like Slipknot or anything, but bigger and bigger – the drums are bigger, the guitars are bigger. And I really like it.'

The single charted at No. 2 in the UK, Ireland, Canada, Denmark and America in addition to doing well in other countries, too.

DID YOU KNOW?

Liam follows more Directioners on Twitter than Harry, Zayn, Niall and Louis do altogether.

DID YOU KNOW?

Once a month the boys have a day they like to call 'Deadly Day'. Louis explained to the *Daily Mail* what it's all about. He said: 'We originally did make it the 22nd of every month as one day where it's kind of more acceptable for us to be, I don't know, just be stupid and run away from everyone, really.'

MIDNIGHT MEMORIES TRACK LISTING:
1. 'Best Song Ever'
2. 'Story Of My Life'
3. 'Diana'
4. 'Midnight Memories'
5. 'You and I'
6. 'Don't Forget Where You Belong'
7. 'Strong'
8. 'Happily'
9. 'Right Now'
10. 'Little Black Dress'
11. 'Through the Dark'
12. 'Something Great'
13. 'Little White Lies'
14. 'Better Than Words'
    Deluxe edition
15. 'Why Don't We Go There'
16. 'Does He Know?'
17. 'Alive'
18. 'Half A Heart'

LIAM'S TOP TWEETS:
'I have been informed that at 11.54 today my fish captain jack black died :(awesome fish, thanks for the 3 years'
'Ive only just heard, thank you so much to everyone who voted for us to win the 2 kids choice awards! Love you all ! Best fans everrrr :)'
'Hope everyone who has seen the tour has enjoyed it, love

seeing everyone there singing along and dancing, amazinnggggg feeling!'

'Andy just beat me 7 1 at FIFA it's his 1st win so he's hyping I must be tired or jet lagged or something so sorry @AndySamuels31'

'I just had monster munch and 2 milky bars for breakfast'

'Im so happy that you all seem to love take me home!! Thank you to everybody whos bought or downloaded it i love you allllll'

'I feel really good today and its a mondayyyy #magicmondays ha watched harry potter yesterday and decided i want to be him ahaa'

'Ha haa andy just wen home on my razor scooter #LankyScooterMan'

'6am already had 3 bowls of frosties'

Why don't you flip over the book and read *Zayn Malik: The Biography*?